Confirmed in a Faithful Community

Catechist's Theology Handbook

Thomas Zanzig

Saint Mary's Press
Christian Brothers Publications
Winona, Minnesota

Nihil Obstat: William M. Becker, STD
Censor Librorum
23 August 1994
Imprimatur: †Most Rev. John G. Vlazny, DD
Bishop of Winona
23 August 1994

The Nihil Obstat and Imprimatur are official declarations that a book or pamphlet is free of doctrinal or moral error. No implication is contained therein that those who have granted the Nihil Obstat or Imprimatur agree with the contents, opinions, or statements expressed.

The scriptural passages cited as NJB are from the New Jerusalem Bible. Copyright © 1985 by Darton, Longman and Todd, London; and Doubleday, a division of Bantam, Doubleday, Dell Publishing Group, New York. Used with permission.

The publishing team for this book included Robert P. Stamschror, development editor; Rebecca Fairbank, manuscript editor; Alan S. Hanson, typesetter; Jayne L. Stokke, Romance Valley Graphics, logo designer; Stephan Nagel, art director; pre-press, printing, and binding by the graphics division of Saint Mary's Press.

The acknowledgments continue on page 180.

Copyright © 1995 by Saint Mary's Press, 702 Terrace Heights, Winona, MN 55987-1320. All rights reserved. No part of this book may be reproduced by any means without the written permission of the publisher.

Printed in the United States of America

Printing: 9 8 7 6

Year: 2003 02 01 00

ISBN 0-88489-343-X

 Genuine recycled paper with 10% post-consumer waste.
Printed with soy-based ink.

Contents

Introduction

The confirmation preparation program presented in *Confirmed in a Faithful Community* includes, not surprisingly, a considerable amount of theological content. Though the program and its content are clearly designed for use with adolescents, virtually *any* discussion of Christian faith and its expression in Roman Catholicism can lead to reflection on and discussion of theologically complex issues. This is particularly true when the intended audience for the material is young people who are often questioning their childhood experience of faith and religion and searching for more meaningful responses to difficult questions. Young people in "searching faith" have a tendency to raise tough questions at the least opportune times; this program actually *invites* them to do so *all* the time! Serving as a catechist for such young people can be immensely gratifying and frequently exciting. It also can be occasionally daunting. This handbook of basic Catholic theology is intended to help support catechists in their challenging role.

The catechist's theology handbook is designed to parallel and complement the preparation process described in the catechist's guide for *Confirmed in a Faithful Community*. The chapters in this handbook follow the basic sequence of the sessions in the catechist's guide. At times, one chapter in the handbook serves as a primary resource for more than one session in the process of preparation. For example, chapter 1 in the handbook is related to the content in sessions 2 and 3 of the period of invitation. Six chapters in the handbook are devoted to the themes covered during the eight sessions of the formation period. I determined the contents of this handbook by asking myself this question: What theological background would best help the catechist work effectively with the specific content of this preparation program? Each chapter, therefore, begins with a brief explanation of how the content of the chapter relates to the material covered in the sessions with the candidates.

All the essays contained here are adapted from two textbooks I developed for use with Catholic high school students: *Understanding Catholic Christianity*, a survey course on basic Catholic doctrine, and *Jesus of History, Christ of Faith*, a thorough study of the Catholic understanding of Jesus and his message. Because those texts were written for an adolescent audience, I struggled to approach the texts' often difficult theological concepts in a style and language that was clear and relatively simple but also theologically precise and accurate. This means that the material presented in this handbook occasionally may seem rather obvious if not simplistic for the more sophisticated adult reader. Remember, however, a primary intent of this handbook—*to serve as a guide and model for how these theological concepts might be presented to young people.* That is, I am not primarily concerned here with explaining the concepts *to the catechist;* rather, I want to help the catechist explain the concepts *to the young candidates.*

Finally, as a collection of essays intended for use as an occasional reference work, the chapters in this handbook do not flow seamlessly one to the other. Nor is the material applied to daily life with anecdotes. The intent is to provide the catechist with the most helpful background information for leading the sessions with the candidates. I trust that such a get-to-the-point approach is precisely what the busy catechist is seeking in a resource of this kind.

As a catechist for *Confirmed in a Faithful Community,* you have taken on an exciting and profoundly important task. I hope you find this handbook a helpful resource as you invite young people into a deeper relationship with the marvelous community of faith we know as the Catholic church.

Tom Zanzig

1

Faith, Religion, and Revelation:
Searching for Answers to the God Question

This essay provides background on major themes treated in sessions 2 and 3 of the period of invitation: "Faith and Religion: Related but Distinct" and "Faith: More Than the Eye Can See." In session 2, you are to make a brief presentation on the important distinction between faith and religion, and then encourage the candidates to explore how those realities have been experienced at different points in their life. In session 3, the candidates expand their understanding of the meaning of faith as a personal relationship with God.

This essay also briefly explores themes that, though not discussed explicitly during the period of invitation, may well be raised in conversation with the candidates in or out of the formal context of the process: the Catholic understanding of revelation and the question of the existence of God. These are pivotal themes that may be of recurring significance throughout the preparation process.

Struggling to Speak of Great Mysteries

An immediate problem encountered in discussions of matters of faith, religion, and revelation is the limitation of words. Finding words and expressions that capture such realities is difficult. What makes the situation even more awkward is that the words we *do* have for these realities are often misused or misunderstood. Take, for example, the implications conveyed by the word *religion.* For one person, the term may mean going to Mass on Sunday. For another, it may be associated with a deep love for Jesus. For a third person, *religion* may mean church teachings about moral issues. For still another, it may summon up bad memories from childhood.

So what happens in a discussion between these people? Suppose that the question posed for discussion is this: What do you think about religion? One person will reply merely that it's all right. Another will respond that it's the greatest experience in his life. A third will say she gets mad every time she thinks about religion. Still another person will say he disagrees with some church teachings but not all of them. Each of these people assumes that he or she knows what all the others are saying. Actually, because each person has a different idea of what the term *religion* means, very little communication is taking place.

In this example, the term *religion* is used to refer to both institutional religious expressions (attending Mass, the church's moral teachings, etc.) and a personal love relationship with Jesus. Many theologians would suggest that the latter would be more accurately referred to as a matter of *faith.* In fact, confusion over these two concepts is a major cause of the difficulties that exist for many people today—old and young alike—regarding their experience of church. Clearly distinguishing between these two concepts is a primary goal of this chapter.

Any discussion of the concepts of faith, religion, and revelation, however, *presumes* one's conviction about a more foundational or fundamental issue—belief in God. After all, without a belief in God any discussion of these concepts seems superfluous if not silly. Surely some of the candidates will be struggling with this issue and may well raise questions about it during open discussion or in private conversation with you. The following discussion provides adequate background to handle such situations.

The God Question

Belief in the loving God proclaimed by Christians presumes the even more fundamental belief in the *actual existence* of God. Some people of high school age may question God's very existence. However, the primary concern of most adolescents will likely center not on the question of God's existence, but on whether to believe and trust in the kind of caring God proclaimed by Christians.

Even believers must admit that undeniable logical proof for believing and trusting in God does not exist, but at the same time, very sound reasons exist for choosing to do so. The following arguments respond to both the foundational question of God's existence and the more complex issue of the actual nature of that God.

Reasons for Believing and Trusting in a Caring God

The following reasons are often given for believing and trusting in God.

The Convictions of Persons Who Care for Us

We can believe and trust in God because our parents and others have taught us to do so. Believing in God is not acceptable *only* because others have taught us to. But this can be a very good reason for initially accepting faith. Candidates should be assured that there is nothing childish or wrong about believing in God "just because my parents taught me to."

Yet mature people cannot rely completely on the word of others as a reason to believe in God. Faith in others can lead us to faith in God, but we must not mistake one for the other. People can let us down. For example, what if those for whom we care choose not to believe and trust in God? Does that mean that we follow their lead away from faith? What about those who are tragically abused by the people close to them? Certainly such victims would seem to have more evidence against faith in God than for it. So we must find other sources of evidence upon which to make a sound decision about God.

Universal Belief in God Throughout History

The vast majority of the world's people claim a belief in Sacred Mystery. It might be argued that they were all taught this belief and merely accept what they have been told. More likely, many of these people find their religious beliefs confirmed in their own personal life experiences. Something beyond their family background and upbringing convinces them of the reality of a god—or sometimes of multiple gods.

Note also that belief in God has been a common human characteristic throughout history. Through sophisticated scientific advances, we are now able to trace the history of human culture back some forty thousand years to the time of the cave dwellers. Throughout history, all cultures have developed religions, with ritual and worship as a part of them. Thus, belief in God—at least as the belief in some power beyond the reach of humanity—is a basic trait of all cultures.

The Wonders of Creation

Another argument for believing in God comes from the order and wonder of the natural world. Today, many people do not respond to the orderliness of the universe so much as to its mysterious qualities and awesome characteristics. We have witnessed a spiritual version of the "back to nature" movement in our society. Many young people, for example, claim that they believe in God but that they more fully experience God while taking a hike in the woods or climbing a mountain than they do in formal worship.

Encourage your candidates to take the opportunity sometime to go outside on a clear, peaceful night and stretch out on the grass. Urge them simply to watch the night sky and let it "speak" to them. They should avoid trying to analyze or understand the mystery and wonder reflected in the stars and just relax and observe. Such moments can be profoundly moving and can expand our worldviews.

Is this experience of the wonders of nature an undeniable proof for the existence of God? Certainly not. The glories of nature may give us, however, an interior, personal sense of mystery that is far more persuasive than highly reasoned arguments. When one considers creation—from the immensity of the universe down to the infinitely tiny world of the atom—and realizes that all of nature holds together somehow, one must ask how . . . or by whom.

A simple Hindu story speaks of what truly seeing the power in nature means:

> "Excuse me," said an ocean fish. "You are older than I, so can you tell me where to find this thing they call the ocean?"
>
> "The ocean," said the older fish, "is the thing you are in now."
>
> "Oh, this? But this is water. What I'm seeking is the ocean," said the disappointed fish as he swam away to search elsewhere. (Anthony de Mello, *The Song of the Bird* [Garden City, NY: Doubleday and Co., 1982], p. 12)

If pressed to explain the tale, the wise Hindu storyteller might express the moral this way: The disappointed fish must come to know that he is not to *look for* something. Instead, he must *look at* the reality that is constantly surrounding him. The same might be said of our search for God.

Moments of Transcendence

Transcendence is a difficult concept to define. Although related to the experience of viewing the night sky, it is more than that. Transcendence refers to the deeply personal experience of moving out from or beyond oneself. For example, the suffering or death of someone whom we know or read about can create feelings of transcendence. In these moments we realize that the world is filled with events that make our personal failures and victories seem trivial by comparison. These compassionate feelings can be powerful enough to lead people to dedicate their life to easing the suffering of others.

All people experience an ongoing yearning for something more in life—as if human beings are always called to reach beyond who and what and where they are and to strive for something better. Most people cannot conceive of their life ending with death. Something more than the desire for self-preservation is at work here. People seem to possess the natural conviction that life is more than just our limited experience of it and that there is a God who sustains it.

The Experience of Love

Moments of transcendence often accompany the experience of love. Love relationships can be profound encounters with the sense of mystery in life. Even the infatuation stage of many love relationships seems to provide us with a sense of the deeper richness and meaning of life. More profound experiences of love—such as a seasoned friendship in which we express a total trust in and care for another person—give us a deep sense of value and purpose in life. For some of us these experiences can stand as proof of the existence of a higher and caring power in the universe.

Almost more remarkable than the experience of loving someone is that of being loved by another. Most people doubt their own value, worth, and goodness. When someone loves us for ourselves, the experience can be indescribably freeing. The gift of another's affection and concern can fill us with a sense of the basic goodness of life and with the belief that such goodness can come only from a gracious and loving creator. By the same token, it is not surprising to discover that lonely, hurt, abused people find that believing in a loving and caring God is difficult at best.

The Lack of Meaningful Alternatives

Explaining the world, history, and our own personal life without a personal, sustaining God seems unreasonable if not impossible. The only alternative is the conclusion that creation was an accident, that the universe is merely an organic machine, and that humanity is headed nowhere. In other words, believing in a caring God seems to make more sense than assuming that life is meaningless.

God, Faith, and Religion

Faith as an Act of Fundamental Trust

The reasons given in the previous section provide a case for believing in God. But, at the same time, a persuasive case can be made against the existence of a caring God, if not against the existence of a God altogether. The suffering of innocent people, natural disasters that wipe out the lives of thousands, the ability of people to be incredibly cruel to one another, the memory of the Nazi death camps, and so on are experiences that haunt believers and challenge religious faith. Faith in God is not always easy. Yet religious faith has stood the test of time and has been lived out in the life of too many billions of believers to be easily rejected.

Some theologians today speak of religious faith in terms of an act of fundamental trust in God. Others speak of faith as a leap into the darkness. Again, religious faith—to the extent of basing the directions of one's life upon it—involves taking a risk on a mystery that we might only briefly glimpse. Those who have taken the risk and made the leap of faith suggest that one can experience the reasonableness of such trust only in the actual act of trusting, that one can come to the conviction that faith makes sense only by taking the risk it demands and then sharing and celebrating the experience with others.

The idea of sharing and celebrating faith brings us naturally to the topic of religion and then to the question of how faith and religion differ but need each other.

The Meaning and Purpose of Religion

When people feel something deeply, they need to express that feeling. For instance, if we want to encourage somebody during an athletic event, we may applaud and cheer. If we care a lot about some people, we may hug them, kiss them, or give them gifts. If we feel angry, we may scream and pound the wall. All these actions are natural and necessary attempts to express inward feelings in outward ways.

This wonderfully human need for expression is part of the experience of religious faith too. Throughout history people have struggled to find ways to express outwardly what they believe about God and what they have experienced by way of that belief. This is precisely what religion is all about. Religion is the attempt by communities of people throughout history to express their shared faith through outward signs—including symbols, celebrations, statements of belief, and codes of behavior. Precisely *how* this is done in any one community depends both on its particular understanding of God and on the available expressions—symbols, celebrations, statements, and codes of behavior—that are recognized and understood by that community. This is the major reason that so many different religions exist in the world even though, at least according to Christian belief, only one God exists.

Faith and Religion: Different but Interdependent

So *faith* and *religion,* in the sense that the terms are being used here, are not the same. Yet they are closely related and complementary realities. In other words, they need each other. Faith—the personal trust in and relationship with God—requires the means of expression that religion provides. Likewise, religion, to have meaning, must arise out of a strong interior experience of faith. If a personal faith is not present, religious expressions have no basis and will eventually become meaningless, empty, and boring.

God and Revelation

If one chooses to believe that no God exists, the discussion about faith and religion could end at this point. If one chooses to believe that God does exist and places religious faith in that God, then, in a very real sense, our discussion is only beginning. For if God does exist, questions such as these immediately come to the fore:

- What is this God like, and how do I discover that?
- How do I personally respond to God, that is, what does God expect of me if anything, and how do I learn about these expectations?
- What kind of religion—that is, religious expression—is the most authentic?
- Is participation in a formal religion necessary, and if so, how do I choose which one to follow?

The answers to all these questions and others like them are rooted in the meaning of revelation and answers to two central questions about it: *How* is God revealed to us, and *what* is revealed to us about God?

The Meaning of Revelation

What is *revelation?* The word literally means "to reveal" or "to unveil." A brief but accurate definition is as follows: revelation is God's self-communication or self-disclosure, in which God reveals Sacred Mystery to people. This definition might answer the question, What is revelation? Yet the two questions posed above immediately come back to mind: How is God revealed to us, and what is revealed to us about God? We can look to our own experience as human beings to gain some hints at answers to these difficult questions and to better grasp the meaning of revelation.

How Does God's Revelation Take Place?

The revelation of God takes place in many ways. As we have seen, the created world itself reveals God to a certain extent. The universe, including our earth, indicates important characteristics of God—as the gracious creator, as the source of all that is beautiful, and as the infinite power behind all that is. God's revelation has also been experienced and understood by people throughout history in four other ways. A brief description of these four ways will be helpful when we later consider how the Catholic community, in particular, experiences and understands God's self-revelation to the human family.

Within individual experience: Some believers understand that the revelation of God takes place within the personal life experience of people. In this view, God communicates directly to and with individuals. This results in a deeply personal sense of union with God. The individual then responds with a whole new outlook and attitude toward life. Both the Hebrew Scriptures and Christian Testament include many stories of individuals' deeply personal experiences of God—for example, the experiences of Moses and Saint Paul. Several Christian churches emphasize the need for this personal religious experience if people hope to gain salvation.

Through the events of history: Other believers feel that Sacred Mystery is revealed through the events of history. In the tradition of Jews and Christians, this is often referred to as *salvation history.* These marvelous events throughout history include the

Exodus and, for Christians, the life, death, and Resurrection of Jesus. Christians speak of Jesus as *the total revelation of God,* a theme to which we will return later in this handbook.

Within sacred writings or scriptures: Many of the major world religions possess special writings that they feel reveal the wisdom of God in unique and holy ways. These writings are called scriptures, which merely means "writings." The Hindu scriptures are known as the *Vedas,* and Islam's holy book is called the *Koran.* Of course, Jews and Christians revere the collection of sacred writings that we call the *Bible.* Exactly how God is revealed in the pages of the Hebrew Scriptures and Christian Testament is a subject of much debate and discussion, and we will return to that question in chapter 2.

Through religious teachings and statements of faith: In this view, a particular religion reflects deeply on the revelation of God—often as it is experienced and expressed through the means previously noted—and then attempts to capture or summarize the core meaning of that revelation in clearly stated teachings of faith. We call such teachings doctrines or dogmas. The particular Catholic understanding of this mode of God's revelation is also discussed in chapter 2.

What Does God Reveal to Us?

A comprehensive discussion of what God reveals to us is more than we can do here. A more detailed discussion of the particular revelation proclaimed in and through Jesus will take place in chapter 4 and, in many ways, throughout the rest of this handbook. In a nutshell, God reveals God's self as the gracious Creator, the Source of All Life, the One who invites us to share in divine life here on earth and in an everlasting way for eternity.

Jesus as the Fullness of God's Revelation

For Christians, the final answer to both revelation questions—How is God revealed and what is revealed about God—is Jesus. God is fully revealed in Jesus and what is to be known about God is to be found in Jesus. The majority of the sessions in the period of formation will be dedicated to exploring these matters in greater depth.

Revelation and Faith

As humans we share the desire to be known by another, to have someone understand us fully. That understanding can only happen, of course, if we choose to let another person into our life. We must take the risk involved in revealing to another those parts of our life about which we are perhaps embarrassed or ashamed. Even in our friendships, we hesitate to reveal our history. As our trust for our friend grows, however, we become freer to reveal our total self. When two people are able to care for and trust each other enough to freely share all that they are as persons, they experience the tremendous gifts of love and true friendship.

The concept of revelation is based on the conviction that God created people in order to enter into a personal relationship in which both parties can fully reveal themselves. God, of course, does not have the fears about being shy or embarrassed that you and I normally have! God's gift of self can be totally free because God *is* God. Clearly God would enter into such a relationship only if God cared deeply for people. So the concept of revelation implies a God who loves and cares enough for people to take the initiative, to become one with humanity in our history, constantly revealing Sacred Mystery to us.

In this context we can understand the Christian conviction that faith is a gift from God. The only way we can ever come to a believing and trusting relationship with God is if God chooses to invite and allow such a relationship. Faith in God can be initiated and sustained only by God.

Revelation and Religion

The notion of revelation is as important to the discussion of religion as it is to faith. The major religions throughout history have developed from attempts by people to understand, communicate, and celebrate what they believe to be God's revelation. As noted earlier, these religions express their convictions about God and the meaning of life through symbols, celebrations, statements of belief, and codes of behavior. Each religious tradition emphasizes different aspects of what it believes is God's revelation as well as what it believes is expected of people in response to that revelation. One religious tradition may emphasize the need for an individual experience of God's revelation, what some would call a conversion experience or a born-again experience. Another religion may emphasize the need to reflect on God's revelation in history and then ritually celebrate those events. Still others may emphasize the need to understand religious doctrines.

A Framework for Understanding Religions

This chapter's discussion of faith, religion, and revelation, along with providing an understanding of the meanings of the three notions, offers an additional benefit. From it a reasonable framework emerges that can guide the study of Catholic Christianity that is at the heart of *Confirmed in a Faithful Community.* As indicated in the discussion, many characteristics are shared by religions in general—namely, a sense of the sacred presence of God and a system of beliefs, symbols, celebrations, and codes of behavior. These characteristics of religion can be organized in a manner that allows us to understand and discuss them in a logical way. For the purposes of *Confirmed in a Faithful Community,* during the period of reflection we will approach our discussion of Christianity and, more specifically, Roman Catholicism in terms of three major components of all religions: wisdom, worship, and works.

Wisdom refers to a religion's basic system of beliefs, what it holds to be true about the nature of God and about God's relationship with the world. The wisdom of Roman Catholicism is embodied in its sacred Scriptures and in its complex systems of beliefs, teachings, and practices. Again, this dimension of Catholicism will be the focus of the next chapter.

Worship includes all the celebrations and communal prayer forms of a religion. Catholic Christian worship, including such areas as the sacraments and the liturgical calendar, is the focus of chapter 9.

Works refers to the code of behavior that is central to the moral teachings of a religion. For Christians, as well as for Jews, this code focuses on the Ten Commandments. More broadly, a certain way of life is expected of Christians—one that includes, for instance, a commitment to act on behalf of justice and peace. The works and spirituality of Catholic Christianity, the primary focus of the period of mission in *Confirmed in a Faithful Community,* is the theme of chapter 10.

The concepts discussed in this chapter—faith, religion, and the meaning of revelation—are so foundational that a brief review of this chapter may be of recurring value in your work with the candidates.

2

The Scriptures
and Tradition:
Growing in Knowledge
About Jesus

This chapter provides background on the Scriptures and Tradition as two ways in which God's revelation is handed down to succeeding generations of Catholics. These two realities are the specific focus of formation session 1, "Learning About God: The Catholic Understanding of Revelation." Given the complex nature of both the Scriptures and Tradition, the treatment of these realities in just a single session is sketchy at best. However, throughout *Confirmed in a Faithful Community,* and particularly during the period of reflection, we will be returning over and over again to these central sources for the Catholic church's beliefs, teachings, and practices. You are therefore encouraged to read this chapter initially to become familiar with its content and then to return to it periodically as relevant questions emerge in your work with the candidates.

The Scriptures: The Word of the Lord

The Hebrew Scriptures

The early church had to struggle with many questions about the relationship between itself and Judaism. However, the value of the Hebrew Scriptures was not debated by the first Christians. These Scriptures, traditionally referred to as the Old Testament, were the only ones available to the early Christian community. Consequently, the church prized the Hebrew Scriptures highly. In fact, Christians believed that the Hebrew Scriptures helped to explain the meaning behind Jesus' life, death, and Resurrection. Early Christians came to believe that Jesus fulfilled many of the passages and prophecies of these Scriptures and that he was the Messiah of whom so many key passages spoke. For example:

- Early Christians knew about Adam, the first man in creation. Jesus was then understood as the new Adam, as the founder of a whole new time and a whole new people.
- The Jews held the Law in extremely high regard. Jesus was then seen as the giver of a new Law. In Saint Paul's writings especially, the Law of Moses is reduced to the commandment to love.
- Jews knew the importance of the Sinai Covenant, the very special relationship between God and the Jewish people. Early Christians then recognized that in Jesus' life, death, and Resurrection a new covenant had been established between God and all people.

The church today continues to recognize the Hebrew Scriptures as the inspired word of God, and readings from it are shared in much of Christian worship.

The Christian Testament

How did the Christian Testament, traditionally called the New Testament, develop? For persons who have been raised in the church, this question may seem a strange one. They may feel that the whole Bible (the word *bible* means "book") was always there. As with all religious expressions, however, the Bible grew gradually out of the life experiences of people as they explored their relationship with God.

Who Is This Man?

Try to imagine the members of the early church drawn together and inspired through the experience of Pentecost. Certainly they were stunned by all that had transpired. They lived with an incredible mixture of joy, confusion, excitement, and fear. What did all these events mean? Jesus was their teacher, but he was obviously more than that—much more. Who was this Jesus who had died and been resurrected?

Although some of the members of the early Christian community were eyewitnesses to the astounding events of faith that were part of Jesus' ministry, only gradually did they arrive at an understanding of who he truly was. As devout Jews they simply could not conceive, as he walked among them, that Jesus was God. This idea would have seemed not only logically impossible to them but religiously intolerable.

In that case, just who did the first disciples of Jesus think he was? Their perceptions of Jesus probably changed and grew gradually as they experienced his life and message. Certainly he was a very special person who spoke with great authority and truth. Only slowly did they recognize and accept him as the Messiah, as the One who was to be sent by Yahweh. The Jewish concept of the Messiah, however, never included the notion that the Messiah was God. The Messiah was expected, rather, to be a kind of special messenger from God.

When did the disciples, then, recognize Jesus as God? They recognized him only after the experience of the Resurrection and after their awakening at Pentecost. Only then were many of the things that Jesus said and did understood clearly for the first time. Only after the Resurrection and Pentecost could the early Christians proclaim, "Jesus is Lord!"

A Time of Reflection

Events of great magnitude require time to assess. In our own life we may spend years trying to comprehend the meaning of marvelous or tragic occurrences. Similarly, the early Christians could not immediately commit their experiences to writing. They needed many years to work through the significance of Jesus' life, death, and Resurrection. So the first Christians gathered regularly to pray and to share stories about the person who had transformed their understanding of life. They tried to remember all that Jesus had said. In doing this, they recognized, often for the first time, the depth of some of Jesus' sayings.

This sharing of intimate memories was not simply a matter of gratification and enjoyment. Rather, the early Christians needed to reassure and support one another constantly as they proclaimed Jesus' message to an indifferent and sometimes hostile world. The first Christians felt driven to proclaim this message—almost literally to shout from the rooftops that, through the Resurrection, "the Lord and Christ whom God has made is this Jesus whom you crucified" (Acts 2:36, NJB).

The Composition of the Christian Testament

How was this message to be preserved and handed on to future generations? For the eyewitnesses themselves, the recalling of Jesus' life and teaching through the discussions and storytelling that we today call the oral tradition was enough. Would this method, however, serve their children or those people in faraway lands who had not yet heard the name of Jesus? Out of this need to preserve the message of Jesus Christ intact, the Christian Testament gradually came to be written. The Christian Testament, as we know it today, consists of the following:

The Gospels: The word *gospel* means "good news." These four accounts of the life, death, and Resurrection of Jesus bear the names of the men traditionally accepted as their authors or editors. Some scholars question whether these men actually wrote the Gospels. They think that other persons may have written or edited the works and then dedicated them to these men. In any case, tradition holds that these men were the four gospel writers:
• Matthew, a tax collector who became one of the Apostles
• Mark, a young disciple from Jerusalem
• Luke, often referred to as "the beloved physician," an educated non-Jew and companion of Saint Paul
• John the Apostle, often called "the disciple whom Jesus loved," who was a teenager when he walked with Jesus and who wrote his very profound Gospel as an old man, after many years of reflection and prayer

The Acts of the Apostles: An extension of Luke's Gospel, Acts depicts life in the early Christian community and the spread of the Christian faith through the travels and preaching of Saint Paul and others.

The Epistles: The Epistles are a collection of twenty-one letters that were written to various Christian communities or individuals in response to a wide variety of problems and needs. The Epistles are organized in the following sequence and are traditionally attributed to the following authors:

- thirteen epistles traditionally attributed to Paul
- one epistle, the Letter to the Hebrews, whose author is unknown
- one epistle by James
- two epistles by Peter
- three epistles by John
- one epistle by Jude

The Book of Revelation, or the Apocalypse: Revelation is a visionary and highly symbolic work. It concludes the Bible and is attributed to John.

Thus the Christian Testament contains twenty-seven small, unique books that were written by different authors and collected together by the church as its Scriptures. The first of these books to be written were the epistles of Paul, which he began composing between 50 and 60 C.E. The last book of the Christian Testament, the Book of Revelation, was written between 90 and 100 C.E. Its authorship is attributed to a person named John, but it is not certain whether this was John the Apostle or one of his disciples. The first firm decision about which books to include in the Christian Testament was not made until about 200 C.E., over one hundred and fifty years after the death of Jesus. In fact, not until this time was the term *New Testament* used for these writings. Nearly eighteen hundred years later, these same Scriptures continue to be the most popular and influential writings in the history of humanity.

Given their frequent use in *Confirmed in a Faithful Community,* we want to concentrate here on the origins, nature, and significance of the four Gospels—those very special books that deal most directly with the person and message of Jesus.

The Gospels: The Good News of Jesus

An Oral Proclamation

Our news-hungry society expects the media to supply information quickly. If a famous rock music star died tomorrow, there would be immediate around-the-clock coverage on television and radio, and a book on the market in a matter of weeks.

Obviously, in Jesus' day these media were not available. So when the disciples experienced the Resurrection, they could not immediately broadcast or publish their reactions. Instead, they began a walking campaign to spread the Good News by word of mouth. Among those who listened, some chose to believe in the message and to gather in small groups to remember Jesus, to share stories about him, to pray together, and to try to interpret the meaning of all that had happened. From these small communities, then, an oral tradition gradually evolved, a tradition that included such elements as prayers that the believers liked to share again and again, and stories about Jesus that would be told repeatedly.

A Spoken Message Committed to Writing

The Gospels were originally committed to memory, not to parchment. They were written down only gradually through a process of collecting and editing the material of the oral tradition. The Gospels as we have them today were not actually written until anywhere from thirty-five to seventy years after the death of Jesus. Even when they were written, they were not intended to be newsy, day-by-day accounts of the life and message of Jesus. Rather, the Gospels were proclamations of the Good News of Jesus by communities of believers.

Belief, by the way, is a critical factor in our own understanding of the Scriptures. Only people of faith could recognize Jesus in his apparitions following the Resurrection. Those who did not believe simply could not see him. The same holds for the recognition of the true meaning of the Scriptures: only a believer will find these writings understandable and exciting.

Also note that each of the Gospels, and each of the Epistles as well, was preached to or written for a particular audience in response to particular needs. Matthew, for example, was writing for the Jewish community, and his Gospel recognizes Jesus Christ as the giver of a New Law that fulfills the Law given to Moses. Luke, on the other hand, wrote for cultured Greeks with their own special perspectives and concerns. As a result, if we are to fully understand the meaning of the Gospels, we need to learn as much as possible about the cultural setting in which each was written.

What Is Not in the Gospels

The need to understand the historical settings brings us to the major difficulty that we confront when reading the Scriptures: we are unprepared for the way in which they are written, and we expect something completely different from what we find. Simply put, the Scriptures are a collection of Middle Eastern religious writings that we read with Western scientific mind-sets.

The implications of this tension are very important for reading the Gospels. Consider, for example, what you would do if you were to write an account of the life and message of Jesus today. What would you write about? What would you include in your book? Because you operate out of a current Western mentality, you would likely develop something along the lines of a biography or a dramatic novel. Specifically, how many of the following items would you include?

- information about Jesus' ancestors and immediate family and the date, location, and circumstances surrounding his birth
- stories about Jesus' youth—the community in which he was raised, activities in which he partook, and information about his physical development and appearance
- a detailed account of Jesus' adult ministry, possibly with a week-by-week commentary on where he went and what he did and said
- in-depth character portrayals of those people closest to Jesus—certainly of his mother and probably of the Apostles
- evidence supporting his claims, his miracles, and the teachings of those who believed in him following his Resurrection and Ascension

You might decide to include most or all of the above items in your gospel account. Yet the fact is that the Gospels offer very little of this kind of information. We do not know from the Gospels, for example, the exact dates of any of the major events of Jesus' life—namely, his birth, the years of his ministry, or his death. We also know virtually nothing about his childhood years. In a similar vein, nowhere are we given even a hint of what Jesus looked like. We have common impressions of his physical appearance, but these are all based on artists' imaginative renderings. We are not even totally sure what Jesus said when he preached. Although we believe that the Gospels, as interpreted in the ongoing Tradition of the church, give a reliable understanding of his message, we are not sure when they contain Jesus' exact words. Can you imagine writing a biography that avoided this essential information? Imagine a news reporter interpreting the words of all the people interviewed rather than quoting them exactly! The point is that the Christian Testament is a very special kind of writing, and our approach to it must take into account its unique character.

Important Reflections on the Scriptures

Given all that we have said so far, several points must be made before closing this brief treatment of the Christian Testament.

Not Just a Book About the Past

Because the entire Bible was written long ago and in a faraway land, we often feel out of touch with its style and its tone. At times we may think that the Bible simply does not relate to us, that it is not relevant. A common complaint among young people, for example, is that the Bible is outdated, that it does not speak to their own needs as they experience them today.

Yet consider the fact that the Scriptures deal with the revelation of a God whose love is always available. That revelation can never be outdated. Moreover, people today seek responses to the same questions and fears that confronted our ancestors—questions about the meaning of life, the fear of loneliness, and the fear of death itself. The Bible speaks directly to these dimensions of human experience.

Inspired by God

Christians recognize and accept both the Hebrew Scriptures and the Christian Testament as products of a loving God revealing Sacred Mystery through the words of human authors. The Bible is commonly said to be "God's book" or "written by God." Often these expressions give the false impression that in the composition of the Bible, God worked independently of people. We can get the feeling at times that the Bible was written in heaven and then simply plunked down on someone's writing desk by a divine delivery service. Actually the biblical authors interpreted their experiences of God in ways influenced by their own personalities and cultures. Yet Christians believe that these authors also wrote with the constant *inspiration* of the Spirit whom Jesus promised. What does the inspiration of the Scriptures mean?

The question of inspiration is both complex and crucial. Its importance becomes clear if one has occasion to meet fundamentalist Christians—Christians who believe that every word in the Bible is literally true. Fundamentalists, for example, believe that the world was created in just six days, as the Book of Genesis states. How do other Christians respond to such a belief if, for instance, they find the evidence for the evolution of the universe over millions of years to be persuasive? Does that mean they disagree with the Bible and therefore are living contrary to the teachings of the church?

The perhaps unnerving response to this question is yes and no. Yes, we may hold some views that are seemingly in disagreement with what the Bible says, but no, we are not necessarily living contrary to its message or the teachings of the church. The basic understanding of the composition of the Scriptures held by Catholic Christians is that the Bible is inspired by God and is therefore without error—here comes the crucial part—in all those things that are necessary for our salvation.

Obviously some things in the Bible are written in the form of poetry or of legends and folktales. Such writings have insights to offer into the wonderful workings of God, but their kernels of truth are in husks or shells that are not essential. To illustrate this, consider which of the following Bible stories and teachings you consider so central to the revelation of God and to the life and message of Jesus that they would be considered necessary for us to be truly Christian?

- All humans are descended from just two people, Adam and Eve.
- All humans are created in the image and likeness of God.
- In the Hebrew Scriptures, a man named Methuselah lived for 969 years.
- Jesus fully revealed to people the nature and will of God.
- Jesus cursed a fig tree and made it wither and die.

- Jesus' message of unconditional love, even of one's enemies, is a basic moral principle.
- The church is guided by the presence of the Holy Spirit to remain true to the essential message of Jesus.

The Catholic church maintains that catching hold of the truth being expressed through a story is more important than believing in every detail involved in its telling.

In other instances in the Scriptures, the truth is being revealed with such directness, authority, and certainty that little or no room exists for indecision or rejection by the reader. For example, in the Scriptures Jesus clearly calls us to care for our brothers and sisters. We ultimately will be judged by God on the basis of our loving response to the needs of poor and outcast people. Jesus Christ's call and our response is central to the entire Christian message and to the church that follows that message.

The examples from the Scriptures that we have chosen to use in this discussion of inspiration are simple ones. What about all those passages in the Scriptures where the meaning is unclear, where a variety of interpretations are possible? How do we decide what to believe about such passages? Of the two responses to this question, the first—given below—deals with the need to study the Scriptures with guidance. The second response deals with the teaching authority of the church, a point we will discuss at some length in the next major section of this chapter.

Proceed with Caution

A major factor in the historic splits between Christian denominations involved scriptural issues—deciding the meaning of certain passages, for instance, or determining who had the authority to settle arguments over these meanings. Because of the tremendous importance of the Scriptures, the Catholic church has always counseled caution regarding the use of the Bible. The disagreements with Protestants, unfortunately, caused numerous Catholic leaders to become overly protective of the Scriptures, and for a long time individual Catholics were not encouraged to read the Bible privately. We have recently seen a tremendous change in this regard, however, and many Catholics today are reading the Bible for the first time, joining Bible study groups, and so on.

This increased interest in the Bible among Catholics is to be applauded and encouraged, but the tone of caution so long associated with the Catholic church is still valid and necessary. At times throughout Catholic history the Scriptures have been used to justify the most unchristian actions. Those who choose to read the Scriptures for personal growth and enjoyment, therefore, should be encouraged to do so with the help of sound study manuals and perhaps in the company of persons who have knowledge and background in the Scriptures. The more central to Christian faith a particular scriptural passage appears to be, the more it deserves thorough study and discussion. The Scriptures are simply too important to be taken lightly or to be interpreted without appropriate guidance.

We turn now to a discussion of the second major way in which God's revelation is communicated to us—the Tradition of the Catholic church.

The Catholic Church and Tradition

The discussion in chapter 1 of the relationship between faith and religion talked about the fact that the inner, personal experience of faith demands the outward, public expressions offered by religion. Certainly the Scriptures reflect this fact. The authors of the Scriptures, guided by God, found powerful and lasting expressions of their faith in the words of the Bible.

In this part of our discussion, we explore other expressions of Catholic Christianity, namely, its official teachings. Earlier, when reflecting on the rich meanings in the Scriptures, we discussed the importance of understanding the nature of the sacred writings, their origins, and their intended audiences. Let's approach our discussion of church teachings with a similar caution. A brief story will help make the point:

> The devil once went for a walk with a friend. After a while they saw a man ahead of them stoop down and pick up something from the street.
> "What did that man find?" asked the friend.
> "A piece of the truth," said the devil.
> "Doesn't that disturb you?" asked the friend.
> "Not at all," said the devil. "I shall let him think that piece is all the truth that there is."

As with most good stories, we had best not analyze or comment at length on this one. Let's simply say this about its message: People struggle to find words for the infinite Sacred Mystery whom we call God. Those words express the truth, but they do not capture it fully. The words are only signposts on the way, not the destination. When the words or statements of belief become the goal or object of our worship, they become hindrances on our path to God. Conversely, when our formal statements of belief point us toward and even lead us to an encounter with God, then they are great gifts worthy of our deepest respect.

With this caution about the limitations of words in mind, let's continue our discussion of the Tradition of Catholic Christianity.

A Definition of Tradition

In *Confirmed in a Faithful Community,* the following is used as a kind of working definition of the church: *The church is the gathering of those people who profess faith in the Risen Christ and his message and who, through the power of the Spirit, live their life in loving service to all people.* Note especially the reference to the Spirit of Jesus in this definition. The Catholic church believes that the Spirit is continually guiding the church, constantly reminding its members of Jesus' powerful message and giving them the insight and courage to live according to that message.

This strong conviction in the constant presence of the Spirit in the church throughout its history has led the Roman Catholic church to believe in what is known as *Tradition.* The term itself is based on a Latin word that literally means "to hand on." So Tradition deals with the handing on of Christian faith from generation to generation through the ages.

Throughout nearly two thousand years of history, the Spirit of Jesus has been with the church as it has evolved. Over those years the church has had to grapple with challenges against virtually every belief that it holds regarding Jesus and the Good News that he proclaimed. In response to each challenge, the church has clarified its understanding of the meaning and implications of that message. In addition, creeds, communal prayers, and forms of worship have emerged, ultimately having as their primary expression in the Catholic church the seven sacraments that we will explore later in this handbook. The Catholic church has developed other religious expressions as well—for example, gestures such as the sign of the cross and genuflection, forms of government for the community, a variety of leadership roles, and so on.

The Catholic church teaches that whenever these gradual developments have resulted in teachings or practices that can be regarded as central to the faithful living out of the message of Jesus, those teachings and practices are then as much a part of God's revelation as are the Scriptures themselves. The essential teachings and practices that have emerged from the ongoing, lived faith of the Christian community are what is known in the Catholic church as Tradition with a capital *T.* Furthermore, the Catholic church believes that the truth of God revealed fully in Jesus is expressed most completely through both the Bible and Tradition taken together.

In the strictest sense, we probably should not speak of the Scriptures and Tradition as if they were two distinct sources of God's revelation. In fact, the Scriptures are themselves one part of the total Tradition of the church, though certainly a privileged part because they record the Tradition closest to the experience of Jesus, who is the fullness of God's revelation. Within the Catholic church, however, the Scriptures and Tradition are customarily spoken of as two distinct ways in which God's revelation is handed on to each generation of believers (although in the end these two ways form a single reality). This distinction helps to clarify the Catholic position on the way God's revelation comes to us in contrast to that of Protestant churches.

Tradition: An Essential Difference Between Catholics and Protestants

Many young people as well as adults raise the question, What is so different about Catholics and Protestants? The reality is that differences exist among all Christian denominations. If that were not the case, we would not have so many denominations! Yet the issue of Tradition is certainly a major characteristic that has identified Catholicism as distinct from most Protestant churches. So the topic of Tradition is vital to our discussion of Catholic Christianity in *Confirmed in a Faithful Community.*

Simply put, a major difference that has existed between Catholics and Protestants is that Protestant churches have placed a central importance on the Scriptures, treating the Bible as the primary, if not the sole, foundation of all their teachings and practices. Often Protestants say, "If it isn't in the Bible, it isn't part of Protestant Christian faith." For this reason, Protestant churches have generally recognized only two sacraments—baptism and Eucharist—because these two are the most clearly identified Christian religious celebrations in the Scriptures. Looking mainly to the Bible also explains why Protestant young people are often much more familiar with the Bible than are their Catholic peers. Religious education in Protestant churches places great emphasis on the learning of biblical stories, the ability to locate certain important passages in the Bible, and so on.

Catholics, on the other hand, accept not only the Scriptures but also Tradition as the basis for their teachings and practices. Catholics believe that as the church moves through history, the Spirit of Jesus Christ guides the church in its ongoing interpretation of the Scriptures and Tradition in its development of particular teachings and practices. On that basis, Catholics accept as parts of God's revelation certain practices and teachings other than those explicitly described in the Scriptures. For example, in addition to baptism and Eucharist, the Catholic church has discerned through Tradition five other liturgical celebrations as being sacraments instituted by Christ—confirmation, penance, marriage, holy orders, and the anointing of the sick—even though these rituals are not as explicitly recognized as such in the Scriptures. Furthermore, Catholic religious education has primarily looked to Tradition, that is, the teachings and practices of the church, as the place to find God's revelation. The Bible was very seldom used directly as a source. Catholics are only recently recovering a strong sense of the importance of the Scriptures, so young Catholics today may still feel ill equipped to discuss the Bible with their Protestant friends.

Since the Second Vatican Council, dialogs between Catholics and Protestants have taken place on a number of controversial issues. Consequently, the sharp distinctions between the Catholic and Protestant approach to the ways revelation is communicated to us are being gradually modified.

Tradition and Traditions

Our normal use of the word *tradition* is so familiar that we might confuse it with the very special meaning of the word in the Catholic church. So a useful distinction can be made here between the church's Tradition and its traditions.

Every community, not only the religious sort, develops customary routines that help to keep the community together and distinguish it from others. The Catholic church has many such customs. For instance, many older Catholics will remember that as children they did not eat meat on Friday. Another past practice was that of using only the Latin language in the Mass. Such customs can, quite obviously, change over time because they are not considered essential to religious faith in the same sense as are more profound teachings and practices such as the sacraments.

The important distinction is this: A teaching or practice that if rejected or lost would distort the essential message of the Gospel is automatically considered to be part of Catholic Tradition. But a teaching or practice that is not recognized as essential to Christian faith is merely a custom that can be changed or eliminated.

This distinction between Tradition and traditions may at first seem trivial. Yet throughout the history of the church, many conflicts between faithful Catholics have focused on whether a particular practice or teaching is essential to faith. Distinguishing between the church's Tradition and church traditions is an ongoing process involving the official teaching authority of the Catholic church, the work of theologians, and the lived experience of the entire faith community.

Who Decides What Is Tradition and What Is Merely a Custom?

Even adult, devout Roman Catholics can be surprised to learn that no single place lists all the teachings and practices that are officially accepted as part of the church's Tradition. With a little reflection, however, the reason for this becomes clear. Despite all that people know about God through revelation, the fact is that God remains a mystery. We cannot hope to neatly or fully describe the infinite God with our words or symbols. We are always just scratching the surface of Sacred Mystery and catching fleeting glimpses of the face of God. For this reason, in the Catholic church's journey through history, its customs and even its understanding of Tradition must be open to growth, refinement, and clarification. To repeat the most important point: Catholic Christians believe that the Spirit is always with the church on its journey, keeping the church faithful to the Gospel of Jesus.

We might still ask: Who leads the church on that journey of faith? Who is to help the church evolve a Tradition that is true to the message of Jesus? The Catholic church identifies three factors that work together to guide the church.

The community of faith: The Spirit of Jesus Christ that ultimately guides the church is present to the entire community of faith, not merely to select individuals within it. Therefore, decisions about which teachings and practices are to be officially recognized as part of the church's Tradition must take into account the lived experience of the entire church.

The theologians: Certain members of the community, by virtue of their education and training, are recognized as valuable sources of information and direction on what is and is not essential to faith. These persons include theologians, whose lifework is to study and reflect on the church's teachings and practices in light of the Gospel.

The bishops and the pope: The Catholic church has always entrusted the authentic interpretation of God's revelation to the bishops in communion with the bishop of Rome, that is, the pope.

The Bishops and the Pope Are Special Leaders

The Catholic church's understanding of the roles of bishops and of the pope is another dimension of Catholic Tradition that makes Catholicism distinct from many other Christian churches. Catholics and a few of the Protestant churches believe that bishops are successors of the twelve Apostles—those special persons who were recruited and taught by Jesus himself. Originally the word *bishop* meant "overseer," and in Catholic history bishops have long been understood to be the primary religious authorities over all the individual churches within geographic regions called dioceses.

The Roman Catholic church is unique among Christian churches in its understanding of the role and authority of the pope. The Christian Testament repeatedly implies that Saint Peter had a special role in the mission of Jesus. After Jesus' death and Resurrection, Peter's role became clearer when he assumed a strong leadership position in the early church—as reflected throughout the Acts of the Apostles. History suggests that later on Peter lived, died, and was buried in Rome, and Christians eventually came to believe that Peter served as the bishop of Rome when he lived there.

Catholic Tradition holds that the current pope is the successor of Peter in much the same way that the bishops are successors of the Apostles. Just as Peter held a primary and central place among the Apostles, so the Catholic church believes that today's pope holds a special role and authority among all bishops. Furthermore, because Peter is viewed as having been the bishop of Rome, the pope of today holds that title and authority as well.

What does this discussion of bishops and the pope have to do with our original question: Who decides what is central to Christian faith and therefore part of Catholic Tradition? The simple answer is that the bishops, in communion with the pope, make these decisions. As previously indicated, however, the pope and the bishops exercise their authority with a sensitivity that takes into account the lived experience of the entire faith community and with the information and advice supplied them by qualified theologians.

Doctrines and Dogmas Are Official Statements of Faith

We have stated that the Catholic church's sense of Tradition includes many dimensions—the sacramental life of the church, various religious gestures and practices, organizational structures, even the Scriptures themselves. In the minds of most people, however, Tradition is most closely associated with formal teachings about faith.

Throughout its history, the church has been challenged repeatedly and sometimes attacked for its basic beliefs. Such conflicts are not surprising, for the message of Jesus Christ is powerful and challenging. That message and the way he lived it ultimately brought Jesus to the cross. So naturally, the church, which professes faith in Jesus and his message, has also faced repeated conflicts with all the cultures in which it has found itself. For instance:

* From its earliest days, the church has had its understanding of Jesus as both God and man challenged.
* The church's positions on various moral issues, such as the morality of war, have often alienated leaders and other people.
* Even practices that are now routinely accepted were heatedly argued at various times. Everything from Sunday worship to

church architecture has been debated and discussed at times in the church's history.

In many cases, conflicts such as these have helped the church by forcing its members and leaders to rethink and refine their understanding of the Gospel in light of the evolving needs of people.

At other times, however, the challenges confronting the church have been of such seriousness that they have demanded an official response by church leaders. Whenever a stated belief is approved as an official church teaching by the pope and the other bishops, it is called a *doctrine*. Furthermore, whenever a specific doctrine of the church is considered to be so essential to the faith of Catholics that any rejection of it would imply a rejection of the faith as a whole, it is called a *dogma*. In the light of all that we have discussed to this point about the Catholic church's approach to revelation, doctrines and dogmas of the church are rooted in the revelation of Jesus Christ as handed on in the Scriptures and the ongoing Tradition of the church.

The Trinity: A Central Catholic Dogma

Many doctrines or dogmas of the Catholic church can be considered central to its identity. For example, the Incarnation of God in the person of Jesus and the church's recognition of Mary as the mother of God are vitally important dogmas for Catholics. As was mentioned, however, no one list exists in which all the official teachings of Catholicism can be found. Yet we must emphasize a particular major dogma of the church, the one shared by virtually all Christian churches, and the one that in many ways is at the very center of all Christian understanding about God. That dogma is the Trinity. You may remember a definition of the Trinity from your past religious education. The most familiar definition is this: The doctrine of the Trinity is the belief that there are three divine persons in one God—Father, Son, and Holy Spirit.

The mystery of the Trinity permeates the Christian Testament. The church's belief in this mystery was present from the very beginning as evidenced by the words of baptism. The dogmatic statement about the Trinity gradually evolved as the church sought to clarify and deepen its understanding of God and to defend its truth against errors that threatened to deform it. In fact, belief in the Trinity was officially declared a dogma about sixteen hundred years ago!

For our purposes, the following insight into the meaning of the Trinity might prove helpful. Saint John in his first Epistle said that "God is love, and whoever remains in love remains in God and God in him" (1 John 4:16, NJB). In what sense can we say that "God *is* love"?

One way to understand God as love is through three elements that seem to be present whenever we experience or witness a deep, honest love relationship.

- One person initiates the love and is the active party reaching out in love to the other.
- One person responds to the love, receives that love, and offers his or her own love in return.
- The actual love shared by the two persons adds an entirely new dimension to the situation. Simply put, when two people love each other, something "extra" is added to the lives of both the lover and the beloved.

If God is love, then God must in some way reflect these three dimensions of all true love relationships. This is what the dogma of the Trinity hints at.

- God the Father is the lover, the one who initiates the love relationship, who reaches out in unconditional love.
- Jesus is the one who totally receives the Father's love—the "Beloved," as the Scriptures speak of him.
- The Holy Spirit, then, is the love shared between the Father and the Son—a love so infinite and unrestrained that it is a power, a person unto itself.

In other words, the Christian understanding is that God is, in a sense, a community of perfect love. In prayerful reflection upon the Trinity, therefore, Christians catch glimpses of the kind of God who is inviting them to share life, and of the love that they are called to share with people, all of whom are born in the image and likeness of God.

Creeds:
Examples of Tradition Contained in Prayer

As noted already, Catholics will not find a complete, clearly stated listing of all the doctrines and dogmas that make up the Tradition of the church. However, the church has constantly sought formulated summaries of its traditional beliefs—often in the context of making professions of faith or in praying and worshiping God as a community. This effort has on occasion resulted in formalized statements of belief known as *creeds,* a term that comes from a Latin word meaning "to believe."

Creeds are not intended to be detailed summaries of every belief held by Christians. Rather, they are essentially prayerful expressions of the believers' shared convictions about the nature of God. For this reason, we should not normally analyze creeds like a theologian or a lawyer who is trying to debate a point of law. Rather, we should pray creeds solemnly, reverently, and sincerely.

The Nicene Creed

The creed most often shared by Catholics in Sunday worship is commonly known as the Nicene Creed because it was first developed in an official church council held in a city named Nicaea in 325 C.E. Think of it: For over sixteen hundred years Catholics and many of their Protestant brothers and sisters have been reciting this creed as a summary of their deepest convictions about God. This special statement of faith serves as a fitting and prayerful ending to this discussion of the Tradition of the church and as a conclusion to this chapter:

> We believe in one God,
> > the Father, the Almighty,
> > maker of heaven and earth,
> > of all that is seen and unseen.
>
> We believe in one Lord, Jesus Christ,
> > the only Son of God,
> > eternally begotten of the Father,
> > God from God, Light from Light,
> > true God from true God,
> > begotten, not made, one in Being with the Father.
> > Through him all things were made.
> > For [us] and for our salvation
> > > he came down from heaven:
>
> by the power of the Holy Spirit
> > he was born of the Virgin Mary, and became man.

For our sake he was crucified under Pontius Pilate;
    he suffered, died, and was buried.
    On the third day he arose again
        in fulfillment of the Scriptures;
    he ascended into heaven
        and is seated at the right hand of the Father.
He will come again in glory to judge the living and the dead,
    and his kingdom will have no end.

We believe in the Holy Spirit, the Lord, the giver of life,
    who proceeds from the Father and the Son.
    With the Father and the Son he is worshiped and
        glorified.
He has spoken through the Prophets.
We believe in one holy catholic and apostolic Church.
We acknowledge one baptism for the forgiveness of sins.
We look for the resurrection of the dead,
    and the life of the world to come. Amen.

3

The Mission Begins:
Preparing the Way of the Lord

This chapter provides extensive information related to the content of formation session 2, "Prepare the Way of the Lord: The Mission of Jesus Begins." That session includes presentations and activities on the nature of the infancy narratives, the baptism of Jesus, and his temptations in the desert—all in 90 minutes. The information provided here about all those events—as well as about Jesus' childhood and, later, his unique relationship with his disciples—is certainly more extensive than what you might need to teach session 2. However, the information is all so fascinating that I had a difficult time condensing it! Also, thoroughly grounding yourself in this background on the life and ministry of Jesus can enhance your comfort level in teaching not only formation session 2 but the rest of *Confirmed in a Faithful Community* as well. So enjoy!

The Infancy Narratives

Both Matthew and Luke began their Gospels with writings about the human origins of Jesus. These writings have come to be known as the infancy narratives—stories about the birth of Jesus and his early life. The Gospel of John, like that of Mark, does not describe the birth or childhood of Jesus. Instead, John's Gospel begins with a profound and poetic statement about the divine origins of Jesus—what it meant for the "Word of God" to become human in the person of Jesus. (See John 1:1–18.)

In the Gospel of Matthew

In the Gospel of Matthew we do not read about the public preaching of John the Baptist or the baptism of Jesus until the third chapter. The infancy narratives in Matthew's first two chapters are an introduction to Jesus' public life.

- The introduction begins with the genealogy, or family tree, of Jesus, tracing his roots back to Abraham (1:1–17).
- The genealogy is followed by the story of Mary and Joseph (including the statement that she becomes pregnant with Jesus "through the holy Spirit") and then a simple description of Jesus' birth and the giving of his name (1:18–25).
- We then learn of the visit of the Magi, or Wise Men, who follow a star to the place of Jesus' birth and present gifts of gold, frankincense, and myrrh (2:1–12).
- The story of the Magi is followed by that of the flight of Joseph, Mary, and Jesus into Egypt as Herod begins to slaughter innocent children, in the hope of eliminating a possible rival to his throne (2:13–18).
- Last, we read of the return of Jesus' family to Palestine and the town of Nazareth in Galilee, where Jesus is to be raised (2:19–23).

These are very familiar scenes to most Christians. The touching images are recalled by families and parish communities each Christmas season.

In the Gospel of Luke

If we look at Luke's infancy narratives about the early life of Jesus, we discover information not contained in Matthew's account.

Luke's preface to the stories about Jesus' birth: Luke begins his infancy narrative with events that happened before Jesus was born, mainly dealing with Jesus' announcer, John the Baptist.

- In Luke's preface we find a rather detailed description of how John the Baptist came to be born to a priest named Zechariah and his elderly wife, Elizabeth (1:5–25).
- The preface is followed by the angel Gabriel's announcement to Mary that she is to bear a son named Jesus, who will be called the "'Son of the Most High'" (1:26–38). (Catholics celebrate this event even today with the Feast of the Annunciation, on March 25.)
- We then learn of Mary's visit to Elizabeth, who is her relative (1:39–45). Upon discovering that Mary is pregnant, Elizabeth exclaims, "'Blessed is the fruit of your womb.'" So in chapter 1 of Luke's Gospel, we find the origin of part of the prayer we now know as the Hail Mary.
- In a prayer now called the Magnificat, we read Mary's beautiful response to the realization that she is to bear a special son (1:46–55). Mary's prayer, which is included in the opening prayer for formation session 2, is actually a collection of many verses from the Hebrew Scriptures.
- Last, we find several scenes centering on John the Baptist: his birth, his circumcision and naming, and a prophetic prayer by his father, Zechariah (1:57–80).

Luke's stories about Jesus' birth and early life: It is only after all of the above information has been shared that Luke begins to describe the birth of Jesus and the events that follow it. Much in Luke's version of these events has found its way into Christmas traditions and therefore into the minds and hearts of most Christians. Some of these ideas are found only in Luke's Gospel.

- Luke offers this familiar description of the birth of Jesus: "[Mary] wrapped him in swaddling clothes and laid him in a manger, because there was no room for them in the inn" (2:7, NAB).

- As noted earlier, in Matthew's Gospel the Magi are led by a star to the place where they find Jesus. But in Luke's Gospel, poor shepherds hear of the marvelous birth from an angel who announces, "'For today in the city of David a savior has been born for you who is Messiah and Lord'" (2:11, NAB). Luke does not mention the Wise Men, nor does Matthew mention the shepherds.
- After telling us of the poor shepherds, Luke describes the circumcision of Jesus, his presentation in the Temple in accordance with the Law, and prophecies about Jesus by a man named Simeon and a woman named Anna (2:21–38).
- Finally, Luke is the only Evangelist to offer the familiar story of Jesus at age twelve when his parents lose track of him during a trip to Jerusalem (2:41–50). They eventually find him in the Temple, "sitting in the midst of the teachers, listening to them and asking them questions, and all who heard him were astounded at his understanding and his answers" (NAB).

Luke's closing statement: Luke closes his discussion of the early life of Jesus with this important statement: "[Jesus] went down with [his parents] and came to Nazareth, and was obedient to them; and his mother kept all these things in her heart. And Jesus advanced in wisdom and age and favor before God and man" (2:51–52, NAB).

The Infancy Narratives and the Christ of Faith

Biblical scholars agree that a great deal of symbolism is involved in the Gospel stories of Jesus' birth and early life. After all, very few people besides Jesus' parents were there to witness the events themselves. In other words, Matthew's and Luke's infancy narratives tell us as much, if not more, about Jesus in light of his Resurrection—Jesus as the Christ of Faith—as they do about Jesus when he walked the earth—as the Jesus of History. The following are the main points Matthew and Luke wanted to teach about Jesus as the Christ of Faith through their infancy narratives.

Matthew's Three Main Points

Jesus is the Messiah. Matthew wanted to show his Jewish readers as clearly as possible that Jesus was the Messiah they had been waiting for. In the genealogy of Jesus at the beginning of his Gospel, for example, Matthew refers to Jesus as "the son of David, the son of Abraham" (1:1, NAB). Then he starts with Abraham and works his way up to Jesus. He carefully notes that Joseph was born in the town of Bethlehem from the line of David. Throughout Jewish history, the people had expected the Messiah to descend from David, and David's hometown was Bethlehem.

Jesus was accepted by Gentiles, rejected by Jews. Matthew included the story of the Magi, non-Jewish men who were members of the priestly caste of the Persians and who served as chaplains to and representatives of the Persian royalty. The Magi were known for their understanding of astrology and the occult, the mysterious dimension of life. (Our words *magic* and *magician* come from the same root word.) By way of the story of the Magi, Matthew was showing his Jewish readers that Gentiles often accepted Jesus as the Messiah even though many Jews rejected him. This theme is repeated throughout Matthew's Gospel.

Jesus is "the new Moses." Matthew filled his entire infancy account with quotes and images from the Hebrew Scriptures, all of which would have had a profound impact on his Jewish readers. For example, in Matthew's Gospel, the Holy Family flees to Egypt, and then an angel calls them out of Egypt to Israel after the death of Herod. Who else was called out of Egypt by God? The Israelites, of course, who were led out of their bondage in Egypt by Moses. So Matthew recognized Jesus as "the new Moses," one who totally fulfilled the Law, the Messiah, who would lead the people to salvation.

Luke's Main Point: The Good News Is for Everyone

Luke had a different audience and a different message in mind as he wrote his story of the birth and early years of Jesus. Though Luke made it clear that Jesus was the Messiah, who fulfilled Jewish hopes and expectations, he did not use a lot of quotes from the Hebrew Scriptures. Luke's readers, who were Gentiles, would not have been as concerned about this as Matthew's Jewish readers. As mentioned before, Luke's Gospel stresses that the Good News is for everyone, especially those who are poor and downtrodden. That was Luke's reason for including the shepherds in his story, indicating that the poor would be the first to recognize and respond to Jesus.

Luke's emphasis on the fact that Jesus offers the Good News to everyone is also illustrated later in a genealogy he offers for Jesus (3:23–38). Luke's version of Jesus' genealogy differs dramatically from Matthew's. Matthew, as noted, starts with Abraham and works his way up to Jesus. Luke, on the other hand, begins with Jesus and works all the way back to Adam. As the "first man," Adam is the father of *all* people, not just the Jews, and with this clever point Luke again affirms the universality of the message of Jesus.

Focusing on the Meaning

When we look at the meaning the Gospel writers were trying to convey, the reasons for the differences in the infancy narratives become clearer. The writers were trying not so much to provide historical facts but to explain the meaning and significance of historical events. In fact, in their infancy narratives, Matthew and Luke may have moved beyond historical concerns altogether, focusing instead on insights into the origins of Jesus that only people of faith would be concerned about.

Certainly we cannot understand any of the events described in the Gospels without asking questions about the meaning of Jesus and his message as understood by the Gospel writers. From this point on—whether in discussing specific events in the life of Jesus, his miracles, or the parables he shared—the constant emphasis will be on the following questions:
• What do these things mean?
• What point were the Gospel writers trying to make?
• What can we understand about Jesus from this?
These questions are at the core of trying to understand the Jesus of History as the Christ of Faith.

The Hidden Years of Jesus' Life

Beyond what Matthew and Luke tell us about Jesus' birth and early years, much of his life prior to his public ministry is unknown to us. The entire period before the start of Jesus' public life is often referred to as Jesus' "hidden years." In addition to the infancy narratives, information about the history of the Jewish people, their beliefs, their religious practices, their family and social life, and so on, can help answer the question, What were the hidden years of Jesus' life like?

With some reservation it can be said that the historical Jesus experienced life as a typical Jew of his day. Note that this claim is made "with some reservation." Jesus was a special person even as a young boy. He must have been particularly gifted, intelligent, and sensitive. This much can be surmised by studying him as an adult.

Jesus: One Like Us in All Things but Sin

Jesus was obviously special, but we must be careful not to think of him as strange, weird, or so different from us as to seem almost inhuman.

In the early church, there were writings and stories about Jesus that did not find their way into our Gospels. One of the stories described Jesus as a young boy who, in order to entertain and impress his friends, would take clay models of birds and magically make them come alive and fly away! Many of us have impressions of Jesus that are not far from this kind of fanciful image. For instance, we might think of the baby Jesus lying in the manger with the power to know all things, to read people's minds, or to go without food and drink. Such images can make Jesus seem like a freak of sorts, rather than what the church has continually claimed him to be—the Son of God, certainly, but also a person who was one with us in all things but sin.

In one of his epistles, Saint Paul says this about Jesus:

Who, though he was in the form of God,
> did not regard equality with God something to be
> grasped.
Rather, he emptied himself,
taking the form of a slave,
coming in human likeness;
and found human in appearance,
he humbled himself,
becoming obedient to death,
> even death on across.

(Phil. 2:6–8, NAB)

Saint Paul is saying that Jesus became as human beings are, with all the physical, emotional, intellectual, and spiritual needs each of us experiences.

Jesus' Birth Date

Our calendar (the calendar of the common era—C.E.) begins with the year 0, marking the supposed birth of Jesus. However, most theologians and biblical historians believe that Jesus was born about five or six years before this date, that is, about 6 or 5 B.C.E. (before the beginning the common era). Thus his birth date can be a bit confusing! The reasons for this discrepancy are too complex to discuss in full here. Basically what happened is this: when our modern calendar was first developed during the sixth century C.E., a miscalculation was made in determining the year in which Jesus was born, and that mistake was never corrected.

We know from the Gospels, however, that Jesus was born during the reign of Herod the Great, and we know with certainty from other sources that Herod died in the year 4 B.C.E. So Jesus was certainly born before that year. Scholars differ on the precise year of his birth, claiming anywhere from 8 to 5 B.C.E. It is obvious that the people of Jesus' day, and the Evangelists, did not share our concern for precise information about such an event. In a typical biography today, one of the first bits of information we would gain about the subject would be his or her date of birth. That detail did not concern the authors of the Gospels at all! So we need not expect to find such information there.

Jesus' Childhood in Nazareth

A Carpenter for a Father

Jesus' hometown of Nazareth was a community of just a few thousand people. He probably lived in the kind of one-room house common among his people. His father, Joseph, was a carpenter by trade, and as was the common practice of the day, Jesus worked along with his father and eventually became a carpenter himself. The carpenter of Jesus' day was a relatively skilled craftsman, and the occupation was a respected one.

A Good Education

Jesus seems to have had a good education. He knew Hebrew, which was fairly rare among the lower-class people of his day. Because of the historical setting in which he was raised, and also due to the location of Nazareth geographically, Jesus probably spoke three languages: Hebrew, Greek, and Aramaic, the common language of Palestine. From age eight to age thirteen he likely attended school in a room attached to the synagogue, where his study revolved around the Hebrew Scriptures and the faith and history of his people, the Jews.

Jesus' education was also enhanced by life in Nazareth itself. Though Galilee was held in low esteem by many Jews, it was an area in which the growing and maturing Jesus would have encountered many of the new ideas of the Greeks and the Romans.

A Faith-Filled Family Life

Ultimately, Jesus' strong Jewish faith had its source and solid foundation in the faith of his parents. Both Joseph and Mary were devout Jews, and the Jewish family was recognized as a religious community in itself. Most likely the family of Jesus was deeply prayerful and committed to faithfully following not only the Law but the spirit of the Jewish religion.

From that early foundation of a strong, loving, and truly religious family, Jesus grew. He developed a profound love and understanding of the Hebrew Scriptures and became fully committed to the personal and communal worship of his people. For some thirty years he "advanced [in] wisdom and age and favor before God and man" (Luke 2:52, NAB).

Jesus was unquestionably a man of deep prayer, as is constantly reflected in the Gospels. He had an intense religious awareness, an understanding of Yahweh and Yahweh's relationship with people that would one day put him in direct conflict with his people, his friends, and perhaps even his family (see Matt. 12:46–50). His vision would eventually lead him to death on the cross, which would offer all people the possibility of fullness of life.

The Beginnings of Jesus' Public Life

John the Baptist was one of the many wandering prophets at the time of Jesus. He was different, however, in that he did not proclaim himself as the Messiah, Savior, or Liberator yearned for by the Jewish people. Rather, he pointed to "'one mightier than I'" (Luke 3:16, NAB). John's task was to prepare the way for Jesus' ministry by calling people to an awareness of their sin and to repentance. He announced that a whole new "kingdom," a new society, was about to begin and that the people were to get ready for it by having a change of heart.

The sign John used to express this change of heart, this openness of mind and spirit, was a ritual bathing called baptism. The act of bathing in water as a sign of spiritual purification was a common practice for many religions of the time, including Judaism. By accepting baptism from John in the Jordan River, people acknowledged both their own sinfulness and their desire to join the new kingdom by changing the way they were living. Later Jesus would praise John, saying that "'among those born of women, no one is greater than John'" (Luke 7:28, NAB).

Jesus' Baptism

Differences Between the Gospel Accounts

All the synoptic Gospels record the baptism of Jesus, and John's Gospel alludes to it, but there are some significant differences between the accounts.

Mark's account: In Mark's account (1:9–11) Jesus is baptized, and then he sees "the heavens being torn open and the Spirit, like a dove, descending upon him." A voice comes from the heavens, saying, "'You are my beloved Son; with you I am well pleased'" (NAB).

Matthew's account: In the account of Matthew (3:13–17) Jesus is baptized only after some disagreement with John about whether John should baptize him. After the baptism, Jesus sees "the Spirit of God descending like a dove," and a voice from the heavens proclaims, "'This is my beloved Son, with whom I am well pleased'" (NAB).

Luke's account: In Luke's account (3:21–22) Jesus is seen at prayer after the baptism has taken place, and it is then that the Spirit descends upon him "in bodily form like a dove." A voice from heaven proclaims, "'You are my beloved Son; with you I am well pleased'" (NAB).

John's Gospel: Unlike the synoptic Gospels, John's Gospel does not describe the baptism of Jesus. However, it does include a passage of testimony by John the Baptist that seems to echo the baptism scenes of the synoptics (see John 1:29–34). This passage also includes some language that is familiar to contemporary Catholics in their experience of the Mass: it is here that Jesus is referred to as "'the Lamb of God, who takes away the sin of the world'" (NAB).

Symbolism in the Baptism Accounts

Certainly some symbolism appears in all of the accounts of Jesus' baptism:
- *The dove:* In ancient times, the dove was often a symbol for Israel as a whole and, less often, a symbol for the Spirit of God.
- *The voice from the heavens:* At times in the Hebrew Scriptures, Yahweh is depicted as speaking to the people in a voice from the heavens. Often Yahweh is concealed by a cloud.

The Evangelists likely used these images to express Jesus' interior experience of God during his baptism. That is, the dove and the voice from the heavens may not have been seen and heard by those gathered about Jesus. Note, for instance, that it is Jesus who sees the Spirit of God descending and that, in two of the accounts, the voice speaks directly to Jesus: "'*You* are my beloved Son . . .'" rather than "'*This* is my beloved Son . . .'"

The Development of the Baptism Accounts

It is interesting to note the development of the accounts of Jesus' baptism from the earliest version (Mark's) to the later versions (Matthew's and Luke's). Mark is straightforward and direct in describing the scene, while Matthew introduces the disagreement with John the Baptist over whether Jesus should be baptized at all. Luke almost skips over the actual baptism and shows Jesus in prayer after the event, and John virtually ignores Jesus' baptism.

Scholars claim that this reflects the Evangelists'—and the early church's—increasing discomfort with the whole notion of Jesus' accepting baptism.

Why Jesus Accepted Baptism

As the early church reflected on the identity of Jesus and grew more and more to recognize him as the divine Son of God, it was faced with this question: Why would Jesus, as Messiah and sinless Son of God, accept a baptism that John the Baptist himself proclaimed was one of "repentance for the forgiveness of sins" (Mark 1:4; Luke 3:3, NAB)? Matthew's statement about John's reluctance to baptize Jesus (3:14) was an attempt by the Evangelist to offer an explanation. According to Matthew, Jesus accepted baptism because "'it is fitting for us to fulfill all righteousness'" (3:15, NAB). That is, Jesus saw the act as part of God's design or plan, and he accepted it on that basis. Matthew wanted to show that Jesus' acceptance was not an admission of sin. Rather, it indicated his willingness to completely immerse himself in the life and concerns of his people, to live as they had to live. For Matthew, Jesus' water baptism was the first step on the road to the cross. (Jesus would later refer to the cross as a baptism he could not avoid [see Mark 10:38; Luke 12:50].)

Jesus' Baptism: A Moment of Self-discovery

The accounts of Jesus' baptism reflect what the early community of faith had come to know and believe about Jesus after his Resurrection, but perhaps they also reveal something of Jesus' growing understanding of himself and his mission. Jesus, like each of us, struggled to find his place in the world. His baptism was apparently a pivotal time of self-discovery, an "aha! moment" in which he came to some recognition of what he was being called to by Yahweh.

Jesus' baptism marked two great recognitions, both symbolized by the writers of the Gospels with vivid biblical imagery:
1. Jesus recognized (as the early Christian community did later) that he was chosen in a special way to proclaim and begin a new kingdom. The words spoken from the heavens echoed those of Isa. 42:1, which told of the "suffering servant of Yahweh" (NAB), who would one day save Yahweh's people.

2. Jesus learned (and the early Christian community realized later) that he would be given the power to fulfill his role through the Spirit of God, represented by the descending dove. That same Spirit of God drove Jesus into the desert immediately following his baptism, and would continue to lead him throughout his ministry.

Jesus' Temptations in the Desert

Mark tells us that immediately after Jesus' baptism, "the Spirit drove him out into the desert, and he remained in the desert for forty days, tempted by Satan" (1:12–13, NAB). The Gospels of Matthew and Luke expand this scene and describe a threefold temptation that Jesus experiences while in the desert (see Matt. 4:1–11; Luke 4:1–13).

In Matthew's Gospel, the tempter, or "devil," asks Jesus first to turn stones into bread, then to throw himself down from a high point of the Temple and have God catch him (in order to prove his special relationship with God), and finally to fall at the feet of the devil and worship him, for which Jesus would then receive "all the kingdoms of the world." In Luke's Gospel, the order of the second and third temptations is reversed, but the content is essentially the same.

According to Matthew's account, Jesus responds to all three temptations by giving direct quotes from the Book of Deuteronomy, which is part of the Hebrew Scriptures. In response to the three temptations, Jesus says, in turn:
1. ""'One does not live by bread alone, but by every word that comes forth from the mouth of God''" (from Deut. 8:3, NAB).
2. ""'You shall not put the Lord, your God, to the test''" (from Deut. 6:16, NAB).
3. ""'The Lord, your God, shall you worship and him alone shall you serve''" (from Deut. 6:13–14, NAB).

Jesus' Priorities in the Desert Experience

Again we must ask, What does this story mean? What were the Gospel writers trying to say about Jesus and his mission?

"The new Israel" did not fail. Each of the synoptic Gospels refers to the forty days that Jesus spent in the desert, and every Jew of Jesus' time would immediately have been reminded of the forty years that the people of Israel spent in the desert searching for the Promised Land. The Israelites were severely tempted in the desert, and they ultimately failed to stay true to Yahweh. Jesus, as "the new Israel," was tempted as well, but he did not fail.

Jesus refused the messiahship expected by his people. A major lesson from the Gospels is that Jesus flatly rejected the political and militaristic messiahship that the Jewish people had come to expect and hope for. The story of the three temptations illustrates this point quite well, for it deals with the kinds of power that Jesus *refused* to exercise throughout his ministry.

- *Economic power:* Jesus' messiahship was not to be based on his ability to provide for the material wants and needs of the people (symbolized by turning stones into bread). Rather, he came to provide for the spiritual hunger of the people by proclaiming the word of God, which offers true life.
- *Magical power:* Nor was Jesus' messiahship to be based on magic and works of wonder that would somehow capture the imagination of the people and almost force them to believe in him (symbolized by throwing himself off the top of the Temple and surviving). Jesus responded to the devil's temptation by saying that God does not reveal divine power through trickery and magic. (Wonder-working would constantly be an expectation of the crowds throughout Jesus' ministry, as we will see in our later discussion of his miracles.)
- *Political power:* Finally, Jesus' messiahship was not to be based on political power (symbolized by the temptation to worship the devil and control all the kingdoms of the world). Jesus said that God alone was to be worshiped and that the Reign of God in the world would take place in the hearts of the people, not in political domination of them.

All three of the temptations we see Jesus confronting—and defeating—in the desert represent the kind of temptations he would have to deal with throughout his ministry.

We must remember that the Gospels were written to guide the early church and its members. The writers, in addition to relaying information about Jesus' ministry, were warning Christians to resist the temptation to find their own meaning and purpose in life through economic security or through personal or political power over others.

The Public Ministry of Jesus: Wandering Preacher, Unique Teacher

Like the Rabbis of His Day

Following his baptism, Jesus became a wandering preacher and religious teacher. It was common for the Jewish rabbis, or teachers of the Law (sometimes called scribes), to roam from place to place teaching. Often the rabbis were accompanied by a band of disciples, young men who freely chose to follow and study under them. It was also common for the rabbis to teach in the synagogues and, less often, wherever people were willing to gather to listen to them—on mountainsides, in fields, or along roadsides. So even though Jesus was probably not a rabbi in an official or legal sense, in many ways his ministry appears similar to a rabbi's.

Unlike the Rabbis of His Day

Several factors—the content of the message he proclaimed, the way he shared it, and his relationship to his disciples—clearly set Jesus apart from the other teachers of his day.

The Content of Jesus' Message

Jesus proclaimed the Kingdom of God. Jesus proclaimed in both his words and his actions the coming of a "new Kingdom of God." The notion of such a Kingdom was a central one for the Jewish people of his day, so it was not surprising in itself that Jesus would speak of it. But his sense of the Kingdom was truly different.

Jesus claimed a special role. Jesus not only proclaimed the coming of a new Kingdom, but he also claimed for himself a special role as the one who would personally establish and embody it, not only announce it.

The Way Jesus Taught

Jesus amazed the crowds not only with the content of his message but with the attitude he possessed while sharing it. As we read in Matthew's Gospel, "the crowds were astonished at his teaching, for he taught them as one having authority, and not as their scribes" (7:28–29, NAB).

The rabbis of Jesus' time were called to study the Hebrew Scriptures and the teaching of other rabbis thoroughly. Whenever they taught they were expected to back up what they were saying with direct quotes from the Scriptures or statements from other respected rabbis.

Jesus, on the other hand, claimed himself as the sole judge of the truth of what he taught. At times he would even say, for example, "'You have heard that it was said to your ancestors, . . . but I say to you'" (see Matt. 5:21–48, NAB). This was a clear break from the common practice, and it both impressed and alienated many people who listened to him preach.

Jesus also differed dramatically from other teachers of his time in his use of parables and in the miracles he performed.

Jesus and His Disciples

The meaning of discipleship: As mentioned earlier, it was typical for a rabbi to attract disciples who would study under him. The disciples would learn from the rabbi in a process of lengthy discussion, memorization through word games, and so on. The goal was for the disciples to learn perfectly the teachings of the rabbi, to the point of being able to repeat his teachings word for word. Once they had done this, the disciples would leave the rabbi and become independent rabbis themselves.

With Jesus and his disciples, however, the relationship was different.

- First of all, Jesus' disciples did not choose him; rather, he called them (see Mark 1:16–20; Luke 5:1–11).
- Second, unlike other rabbis, Jesus did not simply share with his disciples a body of teachings that they were expected to memorize word for word. According to the common practice, one who had mastered all the teachings of a rabbi would in turn be recognized as a rabbi himself and could claim some personal authority on that basis. But Jesus told his disciples that they were not to

take the title *rabbi,* because their only basis of authority came from their relationship with him (see Matt. 23:8–10).

• Third, the disciples of Jesus were not only expected to watch and learn from Jesus, but they were actually called to share in his mission of proclaiming the Kingdom (see Luke 9:1–6).

The special role of the first disciples of Jesus lends insight into what it means to be a disciple of his today. Jesus calls each Christian to a personal, lasting relationship of love with God, and Jesus also sends his followers out to share in his mission of proclaiming the Kingdom.

The Twelve Apostles

Many people responded to Jesus' message and followed him, and all these people might qualify as his disciples. But the Gospels are clear that Jesus carefully selected special men who were to play a central and significant role during his ministry and in the future. These were the Apostles, most frequently referred to in the Gospels as "the Twelve." (Their names are recorded in Matt. 10:2–4; Mark 3:16–19; and Luke 6:13–16.) Curiously, the Twelve are not mentioned in John's Gospel at all, perhaps because John wished to focus more specifically on Jesus himself as the one called to manifest Yahweh's presence and power.

The twelve Apostles and the twelve tribes: The twelve Apostles echoed the twelve tribes of Israel. It is significant that the Evangelists portrayed Jesus as choosing exactly twelve Apostles and that the early community of faith would work to maintain that number after the death of one of them (see Acts 1:15–26). The Israelites at one time consisted of twelve tribes, each descending from one of the twelve sons of Jacob. It seems certain that the early Christian community recognized exactly twelve Apostles to suggest that they would be the foundation of a new community of faith, a new Israel, what we today recognize as the Christian church.

What was so special about the Apostles? The Apostles were, of course, disciples of Jesus. But they were selected by him to be his constant companions, traveling with him from place to place and becoming thoroughly instructed in the truths he shared. The word *apostle* comes from a Greek word meaning "to send forth." Jesus apparently commissioned these men to go out and carry on his Good News about the Kingdom of God. In a special way the Twelve shared Jesus' power, and after his death and Resurrection they continued, in his name, to preach, to heal, and to make disciples through baptism (Matt. 28:16–20).

Ordinary people with an extraordinary calling: What sort of people did Jesus seek for this mission as Apostles? Some were simple fishermen. One was a hated tax collector. Two were such hotheads that Jesus called them "sons of thunder." One would eventually betray him. One was a leader who could show signs of great insight but could also demonstrate outright cowardice. The Gospels often portray these men as dull, baffled, unable to understand what Jesus is telling them. At times they seem to hunger for great power. Eventually they desert Jesus out of fear. In the end, though, all of them but Judas reconcile with Jesus after his Resurrection, and most if not all of these go on to die as heroes in the early church. In short, the Apostles were ordinary people, but because of their association with Jesus, they were capable of extraordinary things.

The Proclamation of the Kingdom

Central to Jesus' identity, his life, his mission and message, and all his words and actions is the notion of the Kingdom of God. Jesus' history as a Jew inspired the notion of the Kingdom. His prayer and life experiences led him to identify himself as the proclaimer and possessor of the Kingdom. His parables pointed to and described the Kingdom, and his miracles were signs of its presence in the people's midst. Therefore, we have to understand what Jesus meant by the Kingdom of God if we are to understand him. The Kingdom of God proclaimed by Jesus is the focus of the next chapter.

4

The Kingdom of God:
Proclaiming
the Dream of Jesus

No concept is more central to understanding Jesus'
life, ministry, and mission than his proclamation of
the Kingdom, or Reign, of God. Formation session 3,
"Jesus' Dream: The Reign of God," is devoted entirely to this theme, and reference to it is made repeatedly in later discussions of Jesus' miracles and
parables, the mission of the church, and other top-
ics. The following exploration of the nature and significance of Jesus' proclamation of the Reign of
God, therefore, will no doubt prove to be helpful
throughout your work with *Confirmed in a Faithful Community.*

The Human Need to Hope

All religions—indeed, all people—reflect a human need to hope for a future that is in some way better than the present. Sometimes such hoping is expressed in a vision of a future society in which all the idealistic dreams of the particular religion are fulfilled. We might call such an idealized picture of the future a religion's *Dream,* with a capital *D.*

A particular religion's Dream will vary depending on what the believers ground their hopes in. For example, a given religion might focus on the military defeat of its enemies. Its Dream would be of a future in which the members of the religion dominate their world with political and military power.

Another religion might be based on the conviction that all its members can experience a deep personal sense of peace. This religion might offer as its Dream a picture of what society would look like if all people attained such inner tranquility.

Jesus, too, had a strong vision of an ideal future, and he dedicated his life to making that future a reality. Jesus referred to his vision as the *Kingdom of God.* Many of his teachings and stories revealed his understanding of the Kingdom. His miracles were expressions of the fact that God was inaugurating the Kingdom through Jesus himself. Jesus' vision came to serve as the driving force for all who would follow him. A full understanding of Jesus— and, therefore, of all Christianity—requires an understanding of the Dream that Jesus proclaimed. The purpose of this chapter is to explore the nature of that Dream.

The Kingdom of God Proclaimed

The word *kingdom* can sometimes get in the way of our understanding what Jesus meant when he preached about the Kingdom of God. For us, the Kingdom of God can automatically imply a place or region. When discussing Jesus' teachings, a better frame of reference might be the *Reign* of God or the *Rule* of God over all of the created world. With this qualification in mind, let's explore what the Kingdom of God meant to Jesus and, therefore, what it should mean to Christians.

The Focus of the Synoptic Gospels

Just as we ultimately turn to the Gospels for an understanding of Jesus, so too we must turn to them for an understanding of the Kingdom of God. In fact, we must look primarily to the synoptic Gospels. Significantly, John's Gospel never explicitly mentions the theme of the Kingdom. John seems to suggest that Jesus himself already embodied the Dream that the synoptic authors describe as primarily a future kingdom. Matthew, Mark, and Luke, then, tell us most directly about Jesus' understanding of the Kingdom of God, and a key part of their message concerns what Jesus did *not* see as the Kingdom.

What Jesus Did Not See as the Kingdom

The Jewish Notion of the Kingdom of God

The basic notion of the Kingdom of God was part of the Jewish worldview with which Jesus was raised. The Jews accepted, for example, that Yahweh was the king over all creation. Many of the Hebrew religious hymns, which we call psalms, celebrated the kingship of God. For example:

> The LORD is king, he is robed in majesty;
> the LORD is robed, he is [encircled] with strength.
> He has established the world; it shall never be
> moved;
> your throne is established from of old;
> you are from everlasting.
>
> (Ps. 93:1–2, NRSV)

So God's kingship was recognized first in the wonders of creation. Some rabbis taught as well that the Kingdom of God was present in the Jewish Law, in the Torah. They felt that the Jewish Law was to be God's instrument for ruling people. The Jews clearly realized that the Kingdom of God had not yet been fully established, because so much evil obviously still existed in the world. They recognized that this was due in large part to their own failure to cooperate with Yahweh, to follow God's will completely.

New Insights into Old Ideas

Jesus certainly accepted much of the Jewish understanding of the Kingdom of God, but he also went beyond it and brought new insights into the older ideas. In some cases he actually contradicted expectations about the Kingdom that were held by the Jews of his day.

The Jews believed that the Kingdom of God would be established through a savior. In the centuries following King David's military conquests, the people's expectation of a savior became bound up with the notion of a new national, political kingship. And by the time of Jesus' ministry, after nearly a hundred years of Roman domination, many Jews expected the Kingdom to begin with a military takeover of the country and the expulsion of the Romans. This overthrow was to be led by the Messiah, who was by then expected to be a military leader, a warrior. Jesus' understanding of the Kingdom and of his messiahship proved to be far different from what his people commonly understood.

Ideas That Jesus Rejected

From the story about Jesus' temptation in the desert—and from all his teachings and actions—it is clear that Jesus rejected specific ideas in the Jewish understanding of the Kingdom. He was certainly not trying to begin a new political reign over his people. In the Gospels, people try to make Jesus a king or political ruler, and he firmly rejects the notion.

Jesus' stand on nonviolence eliminated the possibility of a military takeover of any kind. Clearly, he did not have in mind a geographical state or nation when he spoke of the Kingdom. Jesus' Kingdom would have no boundaries, no borders separating one nation from another. Nor was Jesus' concept of the Kingdom of God simply a new philosophy or a new plan for social reform. But if the Kingdom was none of these things, what was it?

Jesus' Understanding of the God of the Kingdom

Jesus' vision of the Kingdom of God was closely tied to his understanding of God, which differed dramatically from the understanding of God commonly held by the Jewish people.

God as Father

The Traditional Jewish Understanding

Jesus was thoroughly Jewish, so his understanding of the Kingdom of God necessarily flowed out of Jewish history, the Hebrew Scriptures, Jewish worship, and of course, his own personal prayer and reflection on all of these. That personal prayer and reflection led him to a unique and remarkable recognition of God as his "Father." The notion of God as Father was not entirely new to Jesus. The Hebrew Scriptures occasionally used this term for Yahweh. But the Jews held Yahweh in such awe and reverence that they would not even consider using Yahweh's name in prayer and worship. Instead they said "the Lord," "the Most High," or "the Holy One." Calling Yahweh "Father" was definitely out of the question.

Jesus' Name for God

Jesus shattered Jewish belief and practice and took the incredible position of referring to God as "'Abba, Father'" (Mark 14:36, NRSV). *Abba* is an Aramaic word that means something far more intimate than just "father." It was the word used by Jewish children for their fathers; it had the sense of "Da-da," which is uttered so easily by infants. Adults also used the term *abba* as an affectionate term for their father, much as adults of today may continue to call their father "Dad" or "Daddy." In other words, Jesus was saying that people not only could call God by name but could even refer to God with an equivalent of our word *Dad* or *Daddy!* No Jew would have ever dared such intimacy, and it must have shocked many to hear Jesus speak of God with such a sense of childlike affection.

A God Who Loves Without Condition

The Traditional Jewish Understanding

Some Christians unfairly stereotype the Jewish Yahweh as "a God of fear and justice" and Jesus' God as "a God of love." Actually, the Jewish notion of a loving God was very strong. But because the Jewish reverence for God was so great that the people could not even utter the divine name, they often experienced God as distant and removed.

One way the Jews expressed their feeling of distance from God was by referring to God as "the heavens." This explains an interesting expression that Matthew uses in his discussion of the Kingdom of God. Remember, Matthew was writing to a Jewish audience, and he was sensitive to their feelings and religious practices and convictions. Therefore, instead of writing "the kingdom of God," Matthew wrote "the kingdom of heaven." The God of the ancient Jewish people was full of mystery, as demonstrated by the Holy of Holies in the Temple, that sacred place reserved for Yahweh alone.

Jesus' Teachings

Out of his own experience of a profoundly intimate relationship with God, Jesus taught about God's relationship with all people—and indeed with all of creation. That conviction of God's intimate union with all people was a primary part of Jesus' vision of the Kingdom of God. Jesus experienced the nourishing love of God in a deeply personal sense. In the Gospels, Jesus refers often to "my Father," indicating a special relationship that he alone had with God. But he also teaches people to pray to "our Father." Jesus saw God as a passionately caring parent whose love is tireless, healing, unlimited, and unreserved. God offers that love to sinners as well as to the just, to rich and poor people alike, to women and men, to slaves and free people. To the people of Jesus' time, this was a radically new vision, a vision of a God in whom they could place their complete trust. This trust is beautifully expressed in a passage from Matthew treasured by Christians throughout the ages:

> "Look at the birds of the air; they neither sow nor reap nor gather into barns, and yet your heavenly Father feeds them. Are you not of more value than they? And can any of you by

worrying add a single hour to your span of life? And why do you worry about clothing? Consider the lilies of the field, how they grow; they neither toil nor spin, yet I tell you, even Solomon in all his glory was not clothed like one of these. . . .

So do not worry about tomorrow, for tomorrow will bring worries of its own. Today's trouble is enough for today." (6:26–34, NRSV)

The Kingdom that Jesus announced, therefore, was a new understanding of a relationship that God had always offered. In his teachings about the Kingdom of God, Jesus was sharing new insights into the nature of God.

Jesus' Understanding of the Command to Love

According to Jesus, the ability to recognize and fully participate in the Reign of God requires a conversion, a change of heart, a turning from selfishness to openness to God and the call to love. When this conversion happens, the Kingdom of God takes root in the heart of the believer. Jesus' initial call, therefore, is to repentance, to a change in the way we live. Jesus said, "'The time is fulfilled, and the kingdom of God has come near; repent, and believe in the good news'" (Mark 1:15, NRSV).

Not Just "Me and God"

The Reign of God proclaimed by Jesus was not simply a "me and God" situation, a one-to-one relationship between God and an individual person. Rather, Jesus clearly understood the Kingdom as being communal in nature, implying a new relationship not only between God and individuals but *among* individuals. That is, Jesus saw the Kingdom as the rule or reign of God's love over the very hearts of people and, consequently, as a new social order based on people's unconditional love for one another. This meant that an entirely new era in history had begun, a time characterized by peace, joy, freedom, and love.

The Jewish Roots of the Command to Love

Jesus' concept of love for others—like his concepts of the Kingdom and God as Father—was not so much an entirely new notion as an expansion of a notion already held by the Jews. The Jews had such a deep sense of communal love, of concern for poor people, and of generosity that these attitudes had become their identifying traits to the other cultures that surrounded them.

The Ten Commandments, the cornerstone of the Jewish Law, included seven commandments directly related to relationships between people. The giving of alms, or contributions, to the poor was *required,* not merely suggested, by the Jewish Law. And in a touching example of Jewish generosity, the Law forbade the harvesting of corn on the outer edges of the fields so that poor people would have easy access to it. The rabbis even went beyond the basic Law and insisted on attitudes of kindness and gentleness. Over time, however, there developed among the Jews two main problems that conflicted with the command to love others. These were the problems of nationalism and legalism.

Nationalism

The first problem that developed among the Jews was an excessive sense of nationalism. The Jewish sense of separation from all other cultures led some Jews to believe that "love your neighbor" referred to Jewish neighbors only. Some Jews—though certainly not all—even believed that they were called to love their neighbor but hate their enemy. (Jesus refers to this belief in Matt. 5:43: "'You have heard that it was said, "You shall love your neighbor and hate your enemy"'" [NRSV]. But Jesus knows that such a command is never actually stated in the Hebrew Scriptures or in the writings of the rabbis.)

Legalism

Another problem among the Jews was legalism. This was particularly true among the Pharisees. The Jews looked upon the Law as a great gift from Yahweh, a sign of God's love for them. And certainly, some laws are necessary if a society is to maintain any reasonable kind of order. However, over time, minute rules and regulations had developed in Jewish society, not only guiding but dominating virtually every aspect of life. The combination of the Torah (the written version of the Law contained in the Hebrew Scriptures) and the oral teachings of the rabbis, which grew up over the years, led to an extensive system of religious laws. The Torah alone listed over six hundred such laws, governing everything from the Sabbath rest to ritual cleanliness, food and meal preparation, circumcision, and so on. In other words, a basic and decent moral foundation had become overly legalistic and was no longer just guiding the people but actually oppressing them. Saint Paul would have much to say about legalism and the Law in light of Jesus' life and message.

Love Without Limits

Jesus went beyond the limitations of the Law, shattering any sense of narrow nationalism as well as breaking down the barriers of legalism. A particularly marvelous Gospel passage captures this well: In Luke 10:25–37, Jesus asks a lawyer to explain what the Law requires for eternal life. The lawyer responds, as every good Jew would, with the dual commandment to love God and neighbor, and Jesus approves. But then the lawyer presses the issue by asking, "'And who is my neighbor?'" (NRSV). Jesus responds with the thought-provoking story of the good Samaritan. Mainline Jews deeply despised the Samaritans. By telling the story of the good Samaritan in the context of the command to love, Jesus is clearly telling his listeners that they are called beyond the limits of their own Judaism to love *all* people, even their enemies.

The Gospel of Matthew teaches the same lesson:

> "But I say to you, Love your enemies and pray for those who persecute you, so that you may be children of your Father in heaven; for he makes his sun rise on the evil and on the good, and sends rain on the righteous and on the unrighteous. For if you love those who love you, what reward do you have? Do not even the tax collectors do the same? And if you greet only your brothers and sisters, what more are you doing than others? Do not even the Gentiles do the same? Be perfect, therefore, as your heavenly Father is perfect." (5:44–48, NRSV)

Jesus' call to love enemies was unique to him, with no parallel in either the Hebrew Scriptures or the writings of the rabbis.

Love Expressed in Deeds

Jesus did not actually use the word *love* all that much. He spoke more often of the results or expressions of love: service to others, compassion, forgiveness, and reconciliation. For a powerful summary of Jesus' teaching on the law of love, we need only read his familiar story of the last judgment in the Gospel of Matthew: Jesus says that at the end of time, "'the Son of Man'" will offer "'the kingdom prepared . . . [since] the foundation of the world'" to all those who responded to his needs when he was hungry, thirsty, lonely, naked, ill, imprisoned (25:31–36, NRSV). The story continues:

> "Then the righteous will answer him, 'Lord, when was it that we saw you hungry and gave you food, or thirsty and gave you something to drink? And when was it that we saw you a stranger and welcomed you, or naked and gave you clothing? And when was it that we saw you sick or in prison and visited you?' And the king [Son of Man] will answer them, 'Truly I tell you, just as you did it to one of the least of these who are members of my family, you did it to me.'" (25:37–40, NRSV)

According to Jesus, faith in God cannot be lived out apart from service to people in need.

Jesus also claimed that the call to love is a call to unlimited forgiveness, and that God's willingness to forgive people is very much related to their willingness to forgive one another (Matt. 6:14–15). In the Lord's Prayer, Christians pray, "Forgive us our trespasses, *as we forgive those who trespass against us.*" Perhaps if people were more conscious of what they were saying, those words would not come out so easily!

Jesus' Teachings on Love: The Reign of God Made Real

Jesus did not believe that the Law, in itself, was bad. Rather, he recognized that the many spin-offs and additions to it, created by the rabbis and others, had actually crippled the believers' ability to respond to one another with compassion and love. Jesus' challenge to certain dimensions of the Law—for example, the Sabbath laws (Mark 2:2–28) and the laws on ritual cleanliness (Mark 7:14–23)— could not help but alienate many who based their lives on the Law.

The key to comprehending Jesus' teaching about the Kingdom of God, therefore, is in understanding his conviction about the passionate, unrestricted, unconditional, universal love of God—and the power of that love to release and free people to love one another unconditionally, without restrictions. The Reign of God becomes real when God reigns over the hearts of people, and God reigns over the hearts of people when people are in tune with God's will. An often used religious saying is that "the will of God is the good of people." This means that when people conform their lives to God's will, there will be peace, joy, and love for all—that is, the Kingdom of God will be fully realized.

The Reign of God and "the Reign of Sin"

Jesus' understanding of the Reign of God also touches upon one of the most difficult realities of life: the presence of sin and evil in the world. In praying the Lord's Prayer, Christians ask God to "lead us not into temptation, but deliver us from evil." As the Lord's Prayer is found in the Gospel of Matthew, it reads, "'And do not bring us to the time of trial, but rescue us from the evil one'" (6:13, NRSV). In one sense or another, all religions acknowledge the experience of sin and evil in life and offer some response to it.

Sometimes the existence of evil is represented as a supernatural being, such as a devil or Satan. At other times, evil is represented by natural beings. For example, in the story of Adam and Eve in the Garden of Eden, evil is represented as a serpent (see Genesis, chapter 3). In that story, the Scripture writer attempts to explain the presence of evil in the world, while acknowledging that all that had come from God was good. The point of the story is that people are responsible for evil and its effects, because people choose to reject God, not the other way around. Several hundred years after Jesus' death, the church named this historic rupture between God and people *original sin,* the effects of which have been passed down through the ages from generation to generation.

The chief points to recognize here are that sin and evil do exist in the world and that the conflict between good and evil takes place both in the hearts of individual people and in their relationships with one another.

Sin: Both Personal and Communal

Sin can be defined, understood, and experienced in several ways. Catholics commonly think of sin as personal, freely chosen actions that have negative effects on the sinners as individuals and on their relationships with others. But sin can also be understood as a social evil that affects all people simply because we live in community with one another. That is, we can say that the effects of the sinful actions of individual people result in communal sin in which the community as a whole allows sinful conditions to exist or takes sinful action. Communal sin affects all who are born into it. This kind of sin is reflected in the isolation, alienation, and loneliness that afflict so many people today. Examples of communal sin and its effects are war, poverty, and the destruction of the environment.

Evil That Is Not Caused by Sin

Another evil—different from the moral evil associated with and brought about by sin, different from the evil that is chosen—often challenges Christians' basic conviction about the goodness of God. This kind of evil finds expression most readily in the suffering, pain, and often untimely deaths brought about by natural but powerfully destructive occurrences (such as hurricanes and earthquakes) and also by sickness and diseases such as cancer. Such occurrences are not evil in a moral sense but are nonetheless great tragedies for human beings.

There is no simple explanation for, or response to, such tragedies. The ancient Jews thought that even this kind of evil was a sign of personal sin. They believed, for example, that someone suffering from a disease was in some way being punished by God. Jesus did not accept such an explanation. Yet if the message of Jesus was to be truly heard as Good News, he clearly had to say something about both sin and evil, and especially about the power of God in him to ultimately overcome sin and evil.

God Is Ultimately Victorious

Throughout the Gospels we see Jesus encountering the power of personal and communal sin as well as other forms of evil. The constant message of the Gospels is that God in Jesus ultimately does conquer evil in all its manifestations. This does not mean, however, that Jesus did not feel the effects of sin during his lifetime. On the contrary, in his acceptance of the cross he demonstrated his willingness to submit to the effects of sin and evil in their most brutal forms. But God conquered even death by raising Jesus to life in the Resurrection. That is precisely what the Good News is all about—that God is ultimately victorious, that love is stronger than hate, that good always wins out over evil, and that life, not death, has the last say.

The Kingdom of God: Right Now, but Not Yet

In reading the Gospels, we encounter repeated tension, if not complete contradiction, between various claims made about the Kingdom of God. For example, at one point it seems that the Kingdom is very close to us—right around the corner, so to speak (Mark 1:15). At another point it seems that the Kingdom is something to be achieved only at the end of time (Matt. 25:31–46). On one occasion Jesus states that "'the kingdom of God is among you'" (Luke 17:21, NRSV), but on another occasion he tells people to pray for it to come (Matt. 6:10). Three important realizations can be gained from these apparent contradictions:

1. Jesus embodied the Kingdom of God. Jesus believed that the Kingdom was being revealed in his own life and work.

2. Jesus' followers fully recognized the Kingdom only after his Resurrection. God's Reign, as expressed in the life and message of Jesus, was fully recognized by the early faith community only after Jesus' death, his Resurrection, and the sending of the Holy Spirit at Pentecost. This was when the full meaning of Jesus' words and actions became clear to his followers and they began, with the guidance of the Spirit, to understand him and his message in a different light. The entire Gospel presentation of Jesus' life and ministry was shaped by this recognition.

3. Complete acceptance of the Kingdom is required for its fulfillment. One possible explanation for the tension between the "right now" and the "not yet" of the Kingdom is that the power of God was fully present in Jesus and then released to all humanity through Jesus' death, his Resurrection, and the gift of the Spirit. Therefore, the Kingdom of God is close at hand—it is already here in the sense that all the power we need to overcome sin is available to us. But God has chosen to give people freedom, and we individually and collectively have not yet fully accepted the responsibility of making the Kingdom real by living compassionate and forgiving lives. Until all people accept the challenge to love as Jesus did, the Kingdom in its richest sense will not be fully realized.

Jesus' Kingdom Stories and Actions

Ultimately we must confront the sense of mystery that accompanies the coming of the Kingdom of God. The Gospels' language about the Kingdom is so diverse that it is impossible to describe the Kingdom precisely. For example, it may come suddenly, like the unexpected return of a traveler (Mark 13:33–37), or slowly and secretly, like yeast working in bread dough (Matt. 13:33). All the Gospels' variety of language is an expression of a truly wonderful reality: What God can do for people is far greater than anything we can imagine or understand. The vision of the Kingdom—that is, the Dream of Jesus—is magnificent beyond our understanding, yet somehow simple enough that all can respond to its challenge and invitation.

This complex nature of the Kingdom explains, at least to some degree, Jesus' unique use of parables—stories that allow us to catch a glimpse of something that is too big for words—and his striking actions, particularly his miracles. The next chapter explores both of these marvelous dimensions of Jesus' ministry.

5

Jesus Teaches and Heals:
Words and Miracles

Formation session 5, "Jesus Teaches and Heals: Parables and Miracles," focuses on the great teachings and actions of Jesus. The candidates are challenged to look at these elements of Jesus' ministry in a new light, even taking on the role of amateur biblical scholars. Your familiarity with the information provided in this chapter will help prepare you to guide the candidates in their search for a more mature and balanced understanding of Jesus as teacher and healer.

Jesus' Powerful Words

Unlocking Jesus' Words

During his public life, Jesus devoted most of his time to the task of teaching people about his vision of the Reign of God. The title *teacher* is a common one for Jesus in the Gospels, appearing at least thirty times in direct reference to him. Other related titles used for Jesus in the Gospels are *master* and *rabbi.* Different translations of the Gospels use these three terms almost interchangeably.

As noted in chapter 3, Jesus' style as a teacher differed from the traditional style of the rabbis.

- Jesus relied on himself alone as the judge of the truths he shared, rather than depending on the teachings of other rabbis to support his ideas.
- Jesus called his disciples into a lifelong relationship with him and then commissioned them to share in his ministry of spreading the Good News.
- Jesus referred to Yahweh as "Abba," an intimate name for God that did not appear in the Hebrew Scriptures or in the writings of the rabbis.

The first part of this chapter pursues Jesus' role as a teacher a bit further, looking at his words and sayings and, in particular, reflecting on his special form of storytelling: the parables.

To understand the words, sayings, and stories of Jesus, we must keep in mind the vehicle by which they come to us: the Gospels. The Gospels are the early faith community's reflections on and expressions of Jesus' life and message as understood in light of his Resurrection. In other words, we do not find Jesus' everyday, casual conversation in the Gospels. We have, rather, his most significant thoughts and ideas—expressed through the words of those who heard him. In most cases, these words were passed on orally for many years before finally being recorded in the Gospels.

A central key to understanding Jesus' words is to remember that Jesus was thoroughly Jewish, as were most of his followers. He naturally spoke to them with their imagery and speech patterns, and within the context of how they experienced and understood the world.

Engaging the Whole Person

Our own culture has been heavily influenced by the Greek way of thinking. That is, we expect ideas and arguments to be arranged in an orderly manner, and we expect logical proofs for things. But this way of thinking and talking was not common among the Jews of Jesus' day.

For the ancient Jews, the art of speaking was not so much a matter of convincing people through logical formulas, but rather one of establishing contact with the total person—with the listener's emotions and feelings as well as intellect. Thus, the Jewish manner of speaking was far more poetic than our own, filled with a heavy use of symbolism, figures of speech, exaggeration, and so on. For example, Jesus said, "'If your hand causes you to stumble, cut it off'" (Mark 9:43, NRSV). Surely Jesus did not mean this literally but was using exaggeration to make a point as strongly as possible.

Supporting Statements with the Scriptures

In the Jewish tradition, a master of public speaking also filled his presentations with imagery from the Hebrew Scriptures. Virtually every statement had to be supported with the word of God as preserved in the Hebrew Bible.

Jesus demonstrated a thorough familiarity with the sacred writings, and his teachings were filled with references to them. In fact, some of his most striking statements were actually biblical quotes. For example, most of us are familiar with his statement that we are called to "turn the other cheek" if someone strikes us. But this statement by Jesus was actually based on one already contained in the Book of Lamentations (3:30), of the Hebrew Scriptures. Jesus was following a common practice when he taught in this way, though he often gave his own special "twist" or insight when doing so.

A Variety of Sayings

Jesus' teaching and preaching included a variety of styles of speech, but most common were these four: direct pronouncements, short sayings, instructions for disciples, and—perhaps most significant—parables.

Pronouncement Stories

The Gospel writers situated Jesus' pronouncements within stories. A story acted as a setup for a pronouncement, much like a story is told today to get to a punch line. Jesus' "punch lines" contained the main lessons he wanted to get across. Scholars suggest that although the pronouncements themselves may have originated with Jesus, the stories preceding them were situated by the Evangelists to meet the needs of their audiences. This would be one explanation of why a pronouncement by Jesus sometimes appears with different stories in different Gospels.

Pronouncement stories were popular in ancient cultures and were often told about famous teachers. The stories commonly described a scene of tension—for example, the opponents of the teacher posing a difficult question. The teacher, in heroic fashion, would respond with an insightful proverb or statement, demonstrating wisdom superior to that of the opponents. Here are two examples of pronouncement stories used by the Gospel writers:

Picking corn on the Sabbath: In Mark 2:23–28, Jesus and his disciples are seen walking through cornfields, or grain fields, on the Sabbath. As they walk along, the disciples begin picking the corn—a direct violation of the laws restricting work on the Sabbath. The Pharisees confront Jesus on this, and he responds with a story about David and his followers. The scene closes with Jesus saying, "'The sabbath was made for humankind, and not humankind for the sabbath'" (NRSV). The point of the entire episode is to get to that "clincher," a direct and powerfully simple statement about the relationship of the Law to the needs of people. (This pronouncement story has parallels in Matt. 12:1–8 and Luke 6:1–5.)

Responding to a scribe: Another pronouncement story can be found in Mark 12:28–34. There, a scribe asks Jesus which of the commandments is most important, and then the scribe affirms Jesus' answer. The central point of the entire story is Jesus' closing statement—that the scribe demonstrates by his understanding that he is "'not far from the kingdom of God'" (NRSV).

Short Sayings

"Words to the wise": The Jews were very fond of proverbs, short statements that were "words to the wise." These were offered without any story leading up to them. For example, in the Gospel of Mark, Jesus offers this series of short but highly thought-provoking statements:

> "If any want to become my followers, let them deny them-selves and take up their cross and follow me. For those who want to save their life will lose it, and those who lose their life for my sake, and for the sake of the gospel, will save it. For what will it profit them to gain the whole world and forfeit their life? Indeed, what can they give in return for their life? Those who are ashamed of me and of my words in this adul-terous and sinful generation, of them the Son of Man will also be ashamed when he comes in the glory of his Father with the holy angels." (8:34–38, NRSV)

Hardly any scene is set, no story introduces the statements—the stark and challenging words of Jesus stand alone. We can imagine the impact his words would have had on his hearers.

A classic example—Matthew's Sermon on the Mount: Matthew, in writing his Gospel, used an interesting method for pre-senting the short sayings of Jesus. That is, he put them together in a sort of collection. He developed a scene in which Jesus instructs his disciples on a hill, offering them a series of proverbs (see Matthew, chapters 5 through 7). We have come to call this scene "the Sermon on the Mount." Surely it is one of the most popular sections of the Gospels, and one of the most frequently quoted.

An example of the use of short sayings in our day would be the posters of meaningful sayings that have become popular. These posters usually combine beautiful photography with short, insight-ful statements that catch our attention and cause us to think.

Instructions for Disciples

Some of Jesus' teachings are recorded in the Gospels as instruc-tions for those who would be his followers, his disciples. At times, these passages incorporate other forms of teaching, such as the short sayings and the pronouncement stories.

The Lord's Prayer: One example of Jesus' instructions for disciples would be his words on prayer. Both Matthew and Luke include a section on Jesus' teaching about prayer, each section containing a version of the Lord's Prayer, or the Our Father (see Matt. 6:5–15 and Luke 11:1–13). A comparison of the two versions of the prayer reveals some interesting points: For example, in Matthew's version, it appears that words and phrases have been added to Luke's original version in order to make the prayer more useful for communal worship. Some scholars suggest that the Lord's Prayer is really a summary of the entire Gospel message of Jesus, and it may have been the early church's attempt to summarize his major teachings.

Matthew, chapter 10: Matthew, chapter 10, presents another example of Jesus' telling his followers what they can expect of discipleship. It includes a number of statements that Christians may well wish to skip over altogether:

- "'You will be hated by all because of my name'" (v. 22, NRSV).
- "'Whoever denies me before others, I also will deny before my Father in heaven'" (v. 33, NRSV).
- "'I have not come to bring peace, but a sword'" (v. 34, NRSV).

Not easy reading! Fortunately, doom and foreboding is not all that Jesus offers. He also says:

- "'Cure the sick, raise the dead, cleanse the lepers, cast out demons. You received without payment; give without payment'" (v. 8, NRSV).
- "Whatever town or village you enter, find out who in it is worthy, and stay there until you leave. As you enter the house, greet it'" (vv. 11–12, NRSV).
- "'Are not two sparrows sold for a penny? Yet not one of them will fall to the ground apart from your Father. And even the hairs of your head are all counted. So do not be afraid; you are of more value than many sparrows'" (vv. 29–31, NRSV).

The Jewish affection for short, thought-provoking statements is evident throughout chapter 10 of Matthew.

Parables

The parables form a central part of the synoptic Gospels. The word *parable* comes from a Greek word meaning "comparison." The term has been used to refer to a variety of Jesus' sayings, stories, riddles, and so on, but it is probably most precise to reserve it for his special stories about the Kingdom of God.

A parable usually builds from a literary device called a simile. In a simile, two very different things are compared to one another in order to illustrate a point. The word *like* often—though not always—joins the two parts of the comparison. For example, Jesus would say, "The kingdom of heaven is like . . ." and then compare it to a sower in a field, a mustard seed, or the yeast in bread (see Matt. 13:24–33). In concluding the Sermon on the Mount, Matthew offers a parable that sums up the purpose of the entire sermon:

> "Everyone then who hears these words of mine and acts on them will be *like* a wise man who built his house on rock. The rain fell, the floods came, and the winds blew and beat on that house, but it did not fall, because it had been founded on rock." (7:24–25, NRSV, emphasis added)

Let's take a closer look at the use of parables in the Gospels.

A Closer Look at the Parables

The Technique Behind the Parables

The use of parables is one of the most significant characteristics of Jesus' teaching style. He had a way of connecting his points to the everyday experiences of his listeners so that his teaching would be clear to them and easily remembered.

Based on Everyday Life

The basic story elements in Jesus' parables grew out of the land, culture, and family life of his people: farming and shepherding, children playing and adults working at their trades and crafts. Naturally, some of the settings and story elements may seem strange to the modern reader. Knowing something about the land and daily life of the Jewish people of Jesus' time is essential to grasping the meaning of Jesus' teachings. Yet it was precisely because Jesus drew from the common experiences of his listeners that his teachings— and especially his parables—were powerful. When we read the parables today, it is often helpful to find parallels between our experiences and those of the people Jesus was directly addressing. That is, we can translate the parables into familiar language.

Filled with Surprises

In developing a parable, Jesus would take a common occurrence of the day and add a surprising twist to it, such as a surprise ending. These surprises would keep his listeners alert, or catch them off-guard. The idea was to make people think, to stop them in their tracks and get them to reflect on the lessons he was trying to teach. Here are two examples of Jesus' technique:

The parable of the lost sheep: The parable of the lost sheep is found in Matt. 18:12–14 and in Luke 15:4–7. In the story, a shepherd leaves ninety-nine sheep in search of one that is lost, and then rejoices at great length over finding the lost one. Jesus' listeners would have been taken aback by this, because no ordinary shepherd would have considered risking the entire flock for the sake of one sheep.

The parable of the prodigal son: In the popular parable of the prodigal son (Luke 15:11–32), a father's younger son leaves home to go off and spend his inheritance in a wild spree, while the older son remains loyal to the father and continues to fulfill his responsibilities. When the younger son runs out of money, he returns home begging for mercy. What does the father do? He does not start comparing the younger boy with the older one, who remained loyal. Nor does he *reluctantly* agree to take back the wayward son. Instead the father throws a magnificent party for the one who was such a disappointment to him. (Anyone listening to this parable has to be sympathetic with the older son's anger about the situation!)

With both of these parables, Jesus was teaching his followers about God's boundless and forgiving love for those who have gone astray. God's love is so profound that it literally seems to defy common sense!

Themes of the Parables

Chapter 4 of this handbook addressed the central significance of the Kingdom of God in Jesus' message. Not surprisingly, many of Jesus' sayings and stories either relate directly to his proclamation of God's Kingdom or flow out of his own awareness of the complex nature of the Kingdom.

Although it is hard to arrive at a clear-cut breakdown of all the parables, the following organization of the parables into four main themes or purposes is helpful.

Descriptions of God

Some parables describe the King of the Kingdom, namely God. That is, these parables deal primarily with God's nature, qualities, attitudes in dealing with people, and so on.

The parable of the lost sheep: As noted earlier, the parable of the lost sheep (Matt. 18:12–14 and Luke 15:4–7) demonstrates God's gracious love. God takes the initiative and seeks out those who stray.

The parables of the lost coin and the prodigal son: The stories of the lost coin and the prodigal son (Luke 15:8–32) illustrate that God will do almost anything to find us and then will rejoice when we are finally found.

The parable of the laborers in the vineyard: In the parable of the laborers in the vineyard (Matt. 20:1–16), a landowner apparently pays some laborers more than they deserve. Jesus' point, however, is to illustrate the almost overwhelming generosity of God, the fact that God operates out of a completely different "economic system" than the one used by humans.

All four of these parables reflect God in that wonderful image of a Father—the image of a God whom people can call "Abba."

Kingdom Responses

Some of the parables emphasize how we should act if we hope to enter the Kingdom of God.

The parable of the Pharisee and the tax collector: The parable of the Pharisee and the tax collector (Luke 18:9–14) tells us that we should adopt the basic attitude of humility if we are going to participate in the Kingdom. The Pharisee is self-righteous, congratulating himself on his strict religious practices, while the tax collector feels deep sadness for his sinfulness. Jesus says the tax collector is the more righteous of the two because the tax collector recognizes, as all people must, that the need for repentance in life is real.

The parable of the rich fool: In the parable of the rich fool (Luke 12:16–21), we find a man who is self-satisfied because he has grown huge amounts of grain. He plans to build large barns in which to store his harvest. God, however, interrupts the man's planning and says to him, """You fool! This very night your life is being demanded of you. And the things you have prepared, whose will they be?""" (NRSV). This parable illustrates the need to rely on God's graciousness rather than solely on our own resources.

The parable of the talents: In the parable of the talents (Matt. 25:14–30), a man gives each of his three servants a different number of talents, or weights of silver. He then leaves the servants to their own resources as to how they will manage the silver. Two of the servants work to turn a profit with their talents, but one servant fearfully hides his, afraid that he will lose it. Upon returning, the master angrily rebukes this servant for not doing something beneficial with what he has been given. The lesson to Jesus' listeners—and to us—is to make good use of the gifts and talents we have been given, in order to further the Kingdom.

Getting Along Together in God's Kingdom

Other parables address people's relationships with one another and the world at large.

The parable of the unforgiving servant: In the parable of the unforgiving servant (Matt. 18:21–35), a servant begs his master to relieve him of a debt. The master, moved with pity, completely cancels the debt, only to find later that the servant went out and had a fellow servant thrown into prison for not paying a debt owed to him. In great anger the master has the unforgiving servant tortured. The lesson of the parable is that we must truly forgive one another from our heart if we expect to be forgiven.

The parable of the good Samaritan: Though the lesson of the parable of the good Samaritan (Luke 10:25–37) may be clear enough to us today, it was shockingly clear to Jesus' listeners: If people want to be part of the Kingdom of God, they must open their heart to *everyone,* even the outcasts of society.

The Fulfillment of the Kingdom

Finally, some of the parables refer to the future coming of God's Kingdom in its fullness.

The parable of the wedding banquet: In one parable (Matt. 22:1–14), a king is preparing a banquet for his son's wedding. The king sends his servants out to invite selected guests, all of whom reject the invitation. Some of the invited guests even go so far as to kill the servants who deliver the invitation. The furious king has the murderers killed and then sends other servants out to invite anyone they can find. The parable symbolically tells the story of the Jews, who were the first people invited to God's Kingdom. Some of them not only rejected the invitation but actually killed God's servant, Jesus. The "heavenly banquet"—the Kingdom—was then offered to everyone, Jews and Gentiles alike.

The parable of the weeds among the wheat and the parable of the ten bridesmaids: In the parable of the weeds among the wheat (Matt. 13:24–30), Jesus says that the weeds must be allowed to grow together with the wheat, and they will be separated from the wheat at the harvest. In the parable of the ten bridesmaids (Matt. 25:1–13), some foolish bridesmaids get locked out of the wedding banquet because they were unprepared for the arrival of the bridegroom. Both of these parables point to the end time, or the future day of judgment by God.

Understanding the Parables Today

The parables challenge us, as modern readers, to let them speak to our own life situations. We, as individuals and as communities of faith, are called to identify with the lost sheep, with the wicked tenants, with the good Samaritan, and so on, just as Jesus' original listeners were. Here are a few suggestions that can make the reading of the parables more enjoyable and enlightening for us:

1. Look for the central messages of the parables. The details in some of the parables can make the stories more interesting perhaps, but we should not try to read too much into them. The messages of Jesus are often far more direct and to the point than we might expect or recognize.

2. Look for the questions posed in the parables. Jesus sometimes asks his listeners to offer their own response to a parable before he gives his intended message. For example, following the parable of the good Samaritan, Jesus asks his listeners, "'Which of these three [men], do you think, was a neighbor to the man who fell into the hands of the robbers?'" (Luke 10:36, NRSV). Whenever such questions are posed directly or indirectly in the parables, we should pause and attempt to answer them ourselves.

3. Compare our answers with those recorded in the Gospels. Many times the sayings and interpretations that conclude the parables reflect the early faith community's answers to Jesus' questions. It is possible, in other words, that Jesus may not have actually answered some of his own questions or interpreted the parables for the people. Instead, he probably encouraged them to figure out as many insights as they could on their own. As we read the parables, then, we should compare the answers we would give with those given by the early church and recorded in the Gospels. This sets up a kind of dialog between ourselves and the Gospel writers—precisely the kind of exchange that can make the Gospels come alive for us today.

Words into Actions

When trapped by a contradiction between what they profess to believe and the way they actually live, some people fall back on the old saying, "Don't do what I do. Do what I say." A somewhat-related proverb states a similar point: "What you do speaks so loudly that I can't hear what you are saying."

In the case of Jesus, however, there were no contradictions between what he said and the way he acted. All that he said and did
revealed his tremendous vision of the Reign of God over all creation
and in the hearts of people. We have been discussing the words and
sayings of Jesus. But because Jesus spoke *and* acted, no study of
him and his message can be complete without discussing some of
his most challenging and perhaps confusing actions: his miracles.
We turn now to reflection on these marvelous actions of Jesus.

Jesus' Marvelous Deeds: The Miracles

When we read about Jesus in the Gospels today, how do we know
that he was not suffering from delusions, that he was not insane or
perhaps just plain lying when he spoke of the Kingdom? As some
have stated it, Jesus was one of three things: a lunatic, the greatest
con artist in history, or precisely who he claimed to be—"the One
sent by God." What makes his words worthy of our trust?

One significant factor is Jesus' actions. His actions—particularly his miracles, or signs—were as important to his ministry as his
teachings.

Why Are the Miracles So Challenging?

Perhaps no image of Jesus both captures our imagination and challenges our mind more than that of Jesus as "the miracle worker."
Our imagination gets caught up with scenes of power and awe—
people raised to life with a simple word, blindness cured with a
touch, sickness and disease rendered powerless in the presence of
Jesus. These same scenes have moved millions of people to faith
throughout the history of Christianity. Yet the notion of miracles often presents the logical and scientific mind of today with serious,
disturbing questions rather than faith-strengthening signs of hope.
Why might this be so?

Miracles in the Modern World

The way we view the world today is drastically different from the
way the Jews viewed it in Jesus' day. We expect proof, evidence,
and logical explanations for virtually everything we encounter.

The typical responses: Two extreme responses to Jesus' miracles are typical of our time, given our contemporary expectations: people either "take 'em or leave 'em."

- *Take 'em:* Some of today's Christians simply accept all the Gospel miracles at face value. And in doing so, they feel forced to reject many of our modern scientific and biblical findings. These people are often referred to as fundamentalists, and they opt for a literal interpretation of the Bible. That is, they do not accept any part of the Scriptures as symbolic or open to various interpretations.

- *Leave 'em:* At the other extreme, many people—both Christians and non-Christians—reject any possibility of the miracles. Miracles are, by definition, phenomena that go beyond the laws of nature and point directly to the hand of God as their cause. Those who deny Jesus' miracles consider these Gospel accounts as the illusions of a backward people or as fables of some kind.

Another option: Today's Christians can and should hold a middle ground between the two extreme positions on Jesus' miracles. It is not right or necessary, for example, to lump all the miracle accounts together and treat them the same way, giving one as much factual validity or significance as another. But if we get too bound up with whether an individual event occurred exactly the way the Gospels describe it, we risk completely missing the truth that the story can reveal to us. Certainly all these marvelous stories have something true and valid to teach us about Jesus and his proclamation of the Kingdom.

Jesus Did Work Some Miracles

The Christian who takes the middle ground on the issue of miracles can be sure that Jesus did, in fact, work some wonders. Much evidence, and even common sense, upholds this. Consider the following points about Jesus' miracles:

Supported by historical records: Some non-Christian historians of ancient times referred to Jesus as a "wonder-worker." So it is evident from historical records that Jesus greatly impressed the crowds with his actions.

Not denied by the Pharisees: Even the Pharisees in the Gospels do not deny that Jesus worked many wonders. Instead, the Pharisees charge him with doing so through the power of the devil (see Matt. 12:24 and Luke 11:15). Biblical scholars claim that this charge by the Pharisees would have been too unusual, too unexpected, to be included in the Gospels if it were not based on an actual incident.

Affirmed by eyewitnesses: An undeniable historical fact is that many eyewitnesses to the works of Jesus—many of whom were still alive when the Gospels were written—believed so firmly in him and his message that they became committed followers. Many even freely chose to die rather than deny faith in him. Such devotion certainly lends great weight to the claims made about Jesus by the Gospel writers. Also, if the Gospel claims had not been based on actual happenings, serious objections would likely have been raised by the eyewitnesses themselves.

Jesus seems to have worked many wonders. The task of sorting out which miracle events occurred just as the Gospels describe them continues to be a major challenge to biblical scholars, and it is certainly beyond the scope of this program. Again, the major concern of this discussion is to understand the meaning of the miracles.

Understanding Miracles in Jesus' Day

A Different View

One way to understand the miracle stories is to recognize that what we today mean by *miracle* is not what the people of Jesus' day meant by *miracle*.

Faith perspectives: People in our modern Western culture tend to view everything from a scientific perspective. That is why miracles are commonly defined as exceptions to the laws of nature. People in our culture also tend to view God as remote and not particularly involved in the day-to-day happenings of life.

The Jews of Jesus' day, however, viewed the world primarily from the perspective of their faith in Yahweh. To them, miracles were evidence of the presence and power of God. And because the Jews believed that God was always present and powerful, miracles were seen not as exceptions to, but actually as the law of, nature. In other words, though the Jews were naturally awed by works of wonder, they were not terribly surprised by them. They expected God to work that way.

God's power over evil: In the ancient Jewish view, everything was an expression of either God's creative power or the power of evil in the world. The rain and the breeze were the direct results of God's activity—the rain was released through the floodgates that Yahweh opened, and the breeze was Yahweh's breath passing over the earth. On the other hand, all illness—from blindness to leprosy to death itself—was the result of evil. Any cure, therefore, was an exorcism, because it "cast out," or conquered, evil.

More miracles and miracle workers: Given the ancient Jewish view of the world, it is not surprising that the people recognized various events as miracles more readily than we do, even though we might be looking at similar events. We look for logical explanations for everything. The Jews already had their explanation for things they could not understand: those things were the activities of their God, Yahweh, who was demonstrating total control over the universe.

Not only were there more events identified as miracles in Jesus' day, but there were also many more wonder-workers, persons who appeared to have strange powers over people and events. We know from sources other than the Gospels, for example, that other rabbis at the time of Jesus were also considered wonder-workers, able to cure people of their afflictions. Wonder-workers were also commonly found in the Greek culture of the time.

A Different World

Another way to understand Jesus' miracles is to remember the rather gruesome aspects of the world that Jesus encountered, a world very different from the one most of us experience.

Common scenes: The people of Jesus' day had no hospitals and no institutions for those who were mentally ill. Medicine was primitive. It was common to see blind and crippled beggars along the roadways and at the gates of the cities. People with diseases like leprosy were forced to roam in bands throughout the countryside, because they were forbidden to enter the cities. Insane people were chained in caves, and their screams could be heard through the days and nights. And not surprisingly, all of these ill people were banned from worshiping in the Temple.

Cruelty or fear? Our tendency might be to condemn the ancient Jewish society for its cruel treatment of the physically and mentally ill, but we must remember why the society acted as it did. All sickness, insanity, and disease were seen as the direct manifestation of the power of evil. Logically, then, healthy people were terrified of those who were sick, fearful of being contaminated by them. In other words, sheer terror, not cruelty, motivated people to reject and banish those who were in need.

Some Jews even felt that sickness was a punishment from God for personal sins or the sins of one's ancestors. This was a terribly difficult belief for those who held it, however, because it was clear that good people seemed to suffer as much, sometimes even more, than apparent sinners. (Jesus talks about this in Luke 13:1–5, assuring his listeners that those who suffer accidents and other misfortunes do not do so because of their sins.)

The Reign of God, no more evil: If, as most Jews believed, all illness and other human suffering were the result of the power of evil in the world, then common sense indicated that the Reign of God would not be truly present until all these manifestations of evil were overcome. It was precisely this belief about God's Reign that the Gospel writers sought to address in telling about Jesus' life and ministry, especially his miracles.

- Through Jesus, God was destroying evil in all its forms and expressions.
- Because God was using Jesus in this way, Jesus was truly the Messiah, the One sent by God to establish the new Kingdom that the Jews had been waiting and praying for.

Understanding Jesus' Miracles Today

Seeing the Hand of God

Today's Christians do not have to have the ancient Jewish experience or worldview in order to see the active presence of God in history. Likewise, a commitment to science need not blind Christians to the marvels of the universe. In fact, science can provide tremendous insight into the creative power of God.

Some scientists, for example, study the origins of the world or the expanse of the universe and come to a strong conviction that a loving God was the source of it all. Surgeons occasionally claim to experience a miracle in the operating room when a patient survives against all odds. Or we ourselves might spy a single flower blooming in a garden and be overwhelmed with the wonder of creation. Such encounters can give us a hint of the worldview that dominated the minds and hearts of the Jews. Sacred Mystery is present behind or within all our life experiences. Realizing this helps us in relating to the worldview of the ancient Jews.

Miracles, Then and Now

Despite the validity of seeing wonders in everyday life, some of the events that are considered miracles in the Gospels do not have to be seen as such during our time. We understand, for example, the incredible power of the human mind to effect change in the body. We talk about psychosomatic illnesses that seem to disappear when patients' attitudes change. And we know of the remarkable power of suggestion that is demonstrated through hypnosis. These psychological phenomena may account for some, though not necessarily all, of the exorcisms recorded in the Gospels, in which emotionally distraught people are calmed by the strength of Jesus' character.

Other accounts of Jesus' miraculous cures may be explained in part as intentional exaggeration by the Evangelists. Exaggeration was characteristic of the writers in Jesus' culture, who made strong and true points by stretching the historical facts a bit.

But these insights do not explain *all* the miracles of Jesus. Nor do they negate Christianity's solid tradition of accepting miracles throughout its history—a history that Christians believe has been guided by the Holy Spirit, the Spirit of Truth. Ultimately, when trying to understand the meaning of Jesus' miracles, we are dealing with both a faith question and a faith answer.

A Faith Question and a Faith Answer

Christians are not expected to blindly accept irrational claims. Rather, they are asked to recognize and accept the real significance of the miracles—their religious meaning—in light of faith in Jesus. In other words, yes-or-no questions about the historical reality of the miracles are not of prime concern. The question to be repeatedly posed is this: What do the miracles *mean?* And this question can be answered only from the perspective of faith.

The requirement of faith: The requirement of faith for accepting Jesus' miracles was as necessary for the people who actually witnessed these events as it is for us today. Over and over again the Gospels mention that Jesus required belief in him and faith in God before he would cure one who was ill. In fact, Jesus could not cure those in his home region who did not believe in him:

> They said, "Where did this man get all this? What is this wisdom that has been given to him? What deeds of power are being done by his hands! . . ." And they took offense at him. . . . And he could do no deed of power there, except that he laid his hands on a few sick people and cured them. And he was amazed at [the prevailing attitude of] unbelief. (Mark 6:2–6, NRSV)

The Meaning of Jesus' Miracles

Proclaiming the Kingdom

A key to understanding the miracles of Jesus is grasping their relationship to his proclamation of the Kingdom of God. At the core of that proclamation—and therefore at the core of the miracles—are these realities:
- God's promise of unconditional love
- God's commitment to the poor and outcasts of society
- God's complete control over the power of sin and evil
- God's offer of complete reconciliation

Jesus did not just speak of his Father's love. He lived out that love in his actions. Love, not a desire to impress the crowds, made Jesus heal people and work wonders. The Gospels are clear on this: Quite simply, Jesus healed because people needed to be healed. He healed out of profound compassion. In Mark 1:41, for example, he is moved with pity for a leper who begs to be cured. In Luke 7:13, sorrow touches Jesus when he meets the widow of Nain, whose son has died.

Special Signs of God's Saving Power

Kindness was not Jesus' only motive for working wonders, however. In the synoptic Gospels, the most common word used for miracles and cures is *power.* In John's Gospel, the word used most often for these works is *sign.* Jesus' miracles, therefore, were signs intended to show God's power over all creation and, in a special way, over the forces of sin and evil.

As with his parables, grouping the miracles of Jesus according to kind can be helpful for grasping their meaning.

The healing miracles: In the Gospels, we see Jesus relieving people of their physical suffering and even bringing some people back from the dead. Wherever evil and its effects are most directly and dramatically evident in the lives of people—in their suffering, their pain, their death—Jesus heals and restores fullness of life.

The casting out of demons: The extent of God's power is the chief lesson of the exorcisms, in which Jesus casts out evil spirits. The Evangelists are showing us that God, in and through Jesus, can confront the power of sin in its most direct forms and conquer it.

The forgiveness of sins: Many of Jesus' miracles reflect a far deeper and more important level of healing than the "mere" healing of the body. For in the context of his miracles, Jesus frequently mentions that the physical healing of persons is directly linked to their acknowledgment of their sin and Jesus' forgiveness of it. Matthew's Gospel, for instance, tells of some scribes who attack Jesus for claiming the authority to forgive the sins of a paralyzed man. Jesus responds to them by showing them that his authority comes from God:

> "Why do you think evil in your hearts? For which is easier, to say, 'Your sins are forgiven,' or to say, 'Stand up and walk'? But so that you may know that the Son of Man has authority on earth to forgive sins"—he then said to the paralytic—"Stand

up, take your bed and go to your home." And [the man] stood up and went to his home. When the crowds saw it, they were filled with awe, and they glorified God, who had given such authority to human beings. (9:4–8, NRSV)

The nature miracles: The so-called nature miracles reveal the same basic message that the other miracles do: God's Reign over all creation is present in this man, Jesus, and is being revealed to the world through him.
• Just as Yahweh drew order out of chaos in the creation of the world (Gen. 1:1–2), so God in Jesus now overcomes all chaos in the world.
• Just as Yahweh parted the waters of the sea to allow the safe passage of the Israelites (Exod. 14:15–31), so God in Jesus calms a storm and walks on water.
• Just as Yahweh offered the special food manna to his people as they roamed in the desert (Exod. 16:12–35), so God through Jesus multiplies the loaves and fish to feed the multitudes.

For Christians, all miracles are signs of the healing and redeeming power of God's love, a loving power present in and revealed by Jesus. No wonder those who walked with Jesus, who watched him touch people, were convinced that he truly was a man of extraordinary power and force!

The Gospel Understanding of Jesus the Miracle Worker

To be consistent with the image of Jesus portrayed in the Gospels, we must certainly avoid viewing him as some kind of biblical superman or magician. Jesus constantly refused any such designation or image. He worked miracles almost reluctantly and, curiously, often instructed those he had cured to tell no one what he had done for them (see, for example, Mark 1:44). Jesus even became angry with those who actually expected miracles as proof of his power (see Mark 8:12). Why? Because he did not want his miracles to cloud or confuse the far greater and more important reality—that "the Kingdom of God is among you!"

Liberator of the Heart

Once people have faith in Jesus and his message, a real miracle has already begun in their heart. The physical cure they experience becomes an expression of an interior reality, a conversion, a change of heart. The cure of their body represents a deeper, more profound change within them. Therefore, they are liberated not only from lameness but also, for example, from legalism. They are liberated not only from a crippling deformity but also from a closed mind. They are liberated not only from physical blindness but also from the inability to recognize the needs of their neighbors. Ultimately, Jesus liberates people from sin and death to goodness and life.

A Man Full of God

One author has beautifully summarized the meaning of the miracles Jesus performed during his ministry:

We find in the miracle stories, as in other parts of the Gospel heritage, that steady testimony to absolute wholeness and utter genuineness of Jesus of Nazareth. He was a man so close to his God that God's own creative power flowed out of him in healing waves. He was a man so dedicated to God's work that his own fascinating power seemed to embarrass him; at times it seemed to get in the way of his message. But, most of all, Jesus was a man so charged with God's own compassion and love that any cry of pain or confusion drew from him an instant response of healing and restoration. (Donald Senior, *Jesus: A Gospel Portrait* [Dayton, OH: Pflaum Publishing, 1975], p. 131)

On the Way to the Cross

It is difficult to comprehend how someone so powerful in word and deed, and so dedicated to works of love and compassion, as Jesus could become a source of great conflict, an object of hatred and fear. Yet surely no single event in the story of Jesus is more etched into the hearts, minds, and emotions of Christians than his agonizing execution on the cross. How can we make sense of the horribly brutal death of such a powerful and good man? The next chapter will seek an answer.

6

The Cross:
The End or a Beginning?

Formation session 6, "Jesus Rejected: Is Death an End or a Beginning?" includes what I call just a "walking tour" of the Gospel Passion narrative, followed by a discussion of the candidates' understandings of and attitudes toward death. Clearly a 90-minute session cannot hope to achieve great depth in dealing with issues of such profound magnitude and complexity. However, grounding your own understanding of the violent death of Jesus and its meaning in solid biblical theology will enhance your confidence that you are thoroughly prepared to tackle these tough issues. I urge you not only to study but to pray about the content of this chapter, which takes a close look at the events that immediately preceded and surrounded Jesus' death on the cross.

Jesus Rejected

It was probably the year 30 C.E. Jesus was a man of some thirty-five years, and his life was about to end abruptly and violently. He had preached for no more than three years, and perhaps less than one. He had proclaimed good news about a kingdom of love, joy, peace, and harmony. But it had all led to this—the road to the cross.

A Man of Peace, a Source of Conflict

Certainly Jesus was committed to peace, and we are right to remember most strongly his acts of love and compassion. But we must recall as well that he seemed to cause conflict and tension wherever he went. His words were often challenging, even threatening, to his listeners. His behavior often shocked those who witnessed it, for it ran contrary to many of the accepted practices of the time. Consider the following:

- On virtually every important issue of his day—marriage, authority, the role and meaning of the Law, the Temple and worship—Jesus' opinion conflicted with that of most people, particularly with those in positions of power.
- Jesus made the outcasts of society—women, poor people, tax collectors, foreigners, people who were physically or mentally ill—the featured beneficiaries in his message about God's Kingdom.
- Jesus claimed for himself a position of authority above that of both the religious and the political powers of his day.

All of this and much more brought Jesus to a direct and unavoidable confrontation with the Jewish and Roman authorities. He was a very real religious and political threat to the way things were, to religious tradition and political stability.

So in many ways, Jesus' violent end was the price he paid for living a life of love and commitment to the One who sent him. For Jesus, to have lived otherwise would have been not only a betrayal of his Father but also a betrayal of his own Dream, his own vision and values. For Christians, the historical event of Jesus' death is significant—but not just because a man was willing to die for his beliefs. As will be discussed shortly, Jesus' death has a larger, more profound meaning.

The Gospel Accounts of the Passion

The synoptic accounts of the Passion of Jesus are Matthew, chapters 26 and 27; Mark, chapters 14 and 15; and Luke, chapters 22 and 23.

John's account, chapters 13 through 19, is quite similar to the descriptions found in the synoptic Gospels. However, John's account includes an extended discussion of Jesus' last meal with his disciples. A prayerful reading of these accounts would be a great supplement to your preparation for conducting formation session 6.

Understanding the Passion Accounts

As we might expect, the arrest, trial, and Crucifixion of Jesus are the most extensively reported events in the Gospels. (Even non-Christian historians reported that Jesus died by crucifixion.) The Gospels seem keyed to these events, as if everything in the Gospels is intended to prepare the reader for Jesus' execution. Even the writing style of the Passion accounts is much different from that of the Gospels' typical stories and short sayings. For instance, we find many more details in these accounts than in other parts of the Gospels. This is so for several reasons, including these:

- The death and Resurrection of Jesus are at the heart of the Christian story. His Crucifixion had to be very carefully explained to the members of the early community of faith.
- What happened to Jesus was totally contrary to what the people had been expecting for their Messiah. Their desire for a great deal of information about these events would have been natural and intense.
- The Evangelists were writing to and for the early followers of the Risen Jesus. These people faced the threat of almost immediate persecution for their faith in him. The reminder that Jesus had suffered persecution and death would be a constant consolation to them.

The Passion accounts were probably among the first stories about Jesus to take on a consistent form. They may well have been part of the worship of the early faith community even before they were committed to writing.

Reconciling the Differences

We find a lot of detail in the Passion accounts, but we also find signs of editorial work by the Evangelists. Naturally, the Evangelists were trying to provide theological insights into the meaning of the Crucifixion. Matthew's Gospel, for example, is the only Gospel that mentions the eruption of graves at the point of Jesus' death (27:52–53). This may well be a case of symbolic imagery that was added to the basic account of the Passion. Also, the Gospel accounts differ—sometimes a great deal—on a number of other points. By concentrating on what most or all of the Gospel accounts have in common, we can arrive at a reasonably clear idea of the historical facts surrounding the arrest, trial, and Crucifixion of Jesus.

Jesus' Final Days

The Last Supper

All three synoptic Gospels give an account of what has come to be known as the Last Supper. Interestingly, the earliest recorded account of the actual institution of the Eucharist—that is, the blessing of the bread and cup—is found in Paul's first letter to the Corinthians (11:23–26). The attention in the following discussion will be on the three synoptic accounts.

A New Covenant Is Made

As the synoptic Gospels relate, on the evening before he was crucified, Jesus hosted a meal for his disciples, in a room loaned to them by a friend in Jerusalem. He followed the normal Jewish custom of his day, giving thanks to God for the meal. But then he took the bread, handed it to his disciples, and said, "'This is my body, which is given for you. Do this in remembrance of me'" (Luke 22:19, NRSV). Likewise, after they had eaten, he took the cup, saying, "'This cup that is poured out for you is the new covenant in my blood'" (Luke 22:20, NRSV).

According to the Gospels, the Last Supper took place near the time when the Jewish people were celebrating Passover, one of their greatest religious feasts. During the Passover feast, the people remembered how Yahweh had delivered them from slavery in Egypt many years before and how, in gratitude, the people of Israel had pledged their loyalty to Yahweh. Ever since that time they had been known as "the People of the Covenant." Thus, when Jesus identified his actions as representing a "new covenant," he was linking those actions to a reality that was at the heart of Jewish history.

"Do This in Remembrance of Me"

Jesus' words and actions at the Last Supper were packed with meaning. The synoptic Gospels suggest these main two points:
- Jesus had his approaching death in mind as he gathered his disciples for that meal.
- Jesus made a real connection between the meal itself and his death on the cross.

When Jesus stood up to do his customary duty as host in saying the blessing over the cup and bread, he startled his disciples by saying that the cup and bread were to be recognized as signs of his own death. At the time, the disciples did not understand what he was talking about. They believed that he had come to Jerusalem to assume his role as king, not to die!

Only later—after Jesus' death and Resurrection—did the early community of faith recall that meal and begin to use the words and gestures of Jesus as a continuing reminder of his death. Nearly two thousand years later, Christians all over the world gather in their communities, solemnly repeating those words and gestures— still recalling in this special way the life, death, and Resurrection of Jesus. Christians continue to "do this in remembrance" of him.

Is Jesus Really There?

It is significant that the various Christian churches today have differing convictions about the way in which the Risen Jesus is present in the consecrated bread and wine of the Eucharist. On the one hand, some Christians believe that the blessing of the bread and wine today is done only in memory of what Jesus did nearly two thousand years ago. That is, the blessed bread and cup are but symbols of Jesus' risen presence within the community. On the other hand, Roman Catholics are firm in their conviction that the Risen Jesus is truly and fully present in the consecrated bread and wine of the Eucharist.

The Agony in the Garden

At some time or another, each of us has felt the terrible ache of loneliness, the feeling that no one understands or cares about us. Perhaps it is because we all have felt this pain that the image of Jesus in the garden of Gethsemane can touch us so deeply.

We might try somehow to soften the pain of Jesus at Gethsemane with thoughts of how, as the Son of God, he could heroically accept the pain of his impending death, sure in the knowledge that his Resurrection awaited him. But the Gospels are clear on this: Jesus' agony in the garden was a time of sheer human terror and darkness. He knew the time was fast approaching when all the conflicts surrounding him would build to a breaking point.

Jesus Could Read the Signs of the Times

Toward the end of his life, did Jesus have a premonition or expectation that he was about to die? We do not have to imagine some interior revelation by God on this, some mysterious inner voice that permitted Jesus to foresee the future. For Jesus could read the signs of the times. That is, he could look at what was happening around him and put all the pieces together.

The building hostility: Jesus was definitely aware of the building hostility of all the people who opposed him, which included nearly every faction of Judaism—Pharisees, Sadducees, Zealots. In a rare situation indeed, all the leaders who normally conflicted with one another were united against Jesus.

The situation in Jerusalem: Jesus had freely chosen to go to Jerusalem. He probably realized that great tension, if not violence, would result from his presence there. Scholars dispute the historical accuracy of some of the details of the Gospel accounts of Jesus' triumphant entry into Jerusalem (remembered today on Passion Sunday, or Palm Sunday). However, it is reasonable to assume that Jesus' arrival in the holy city did cause some sort of stir. And Jesus would have been aware that the authorities—both Jewish and Roman—would not tolerate such emotionally charged happenings during the already intense season of Passover.

The fate of a prophet: Jesus probably recognized himself as a true prophet of Israel, as one led by the Spirit. He knew the history of his people and the way they had treated their prophets. Because Israel had repeatedly rejected the prophets, Jesus would have had a growing expectation of his own rejection as well. At one point earlier in his ministry, he had cried out over the city of David, "'Jerusalem, Jerusalem, you who kill the prophets and stone those sent to you . . .'" (Matt. 23:37, NAB). Jesus would have seen at least the possibility, if not the likelihood, of his having to suffer and even die for his proclamation of the Kingdom.

The faithful love of Yahweh: Throughout their history, the Jews had recognized a strong link between death and victory, between despair and hope. Their experience as a people had led them to realize that often Yahweh was most with them in times of despair—that somehow the greater their suffering, the more vividly was Yahweh's love revealed to them. Jesus was certainly aware of this tradition and must have drawn strength from it.

He Could Have Run Away

In the face of all the evidence pointing to the possibility of a violent death, Jesus could have run away. This would seem to have been the most human thing to do. Yet Jesus stayed—not so much because he knew that God could raise him from the dead, but because he was firmly committed to doing the will of the One who sent him: "'Abba, Father, for you all things are possible; remove this cup [death] from me; *yet, not what I want, but what you want*'" (Mark 14:36, NRSV, emphasis added).

Jesus' free acceptance of his death is central to all of Christian theology. The entire Good News crumbles if Jesus is seen as a dreamer who was somehow fooled by circumstances; or as someone who would have betrayed his convictions by running away, had he known what was coming; or even as someone who knew with absolute certainty that he would be raised from the dead in three days.

The account of Jesus' agony at Gethsemane is a dramatic departure from other stories of martyrs that were popular among the Jews during and before the time of Jesus. In those stories, as in many of our modern TV shows and movies, the martyr faced death with courage and firm resignation, hardly showing a sign of fear. Jesus, however, was no such fictional character, no actor playing out a dramatic role. He was totally immersed in our human experience and, like us, felt loneliness and fear. But he found—as do many of his followers—consolation, strength, ultimate hope, in the one he called "Abba," his Father. And it was in his commitment to his Father's will that Jesus found the courage to accept what was to come.

Jesus' Final Hours

The Trial at the Sanhedrin

At the Great Sanhedrin, the Jewish aristocracy met as a "court of inquiry" to determine what charge to level against Jesus in the trial to be held before the Romans. Although the Jewish leaders clearly wanted Jesus dead, they did not have the authority to carry out the death penalty while they were under Roman control.

The Fateful Question

During Jesus' confrontation with the Sanhedrin, Caiaphas, the high priest, asked the question that—along with Jesus' answer—would eventually lead to Jesus' execution. Caiaphas, becoming frustrated with Jesus' refusal to answer the questions of the other priests, asked Jesus directly, "'Are you the Messiah, the Son of the Blessed One [God]?'" (Mark 14:61, NRSV). Jesus answered:

> "I am; and
> 'you will see the Son of Man
> seated at the right hand of the Power,'
> and 'coming with the clouds of heaven.'"
>
> (Mark 14:62, NRSV)

In this scene, Jesus not only accepts the title *Messiah* (*Christ*) from Caiaphas, but even expands that to say that he is uniquely in touch with divinity, with God. Jesus' response draws an immediate charge of blasphemy from Caiaphas (Mark 14:63–65). (For parallel scenes of Jesus before the Sanhedrin, see Matt. 26:57–68 and Luke 22:66–71.)

A Charge That Would Stick

Blasphemy means "showing a lack of reverence toward God" or, more specifically in Jesus' case, "claiming for oneself a dignity due to God alone." It was not Jesus' claim of being the Messiah that gave rise to the furor among the Jewish leaders. Other men had made that claim before him, and others would make it after his death. According to the Gospel accounts, what totally shocked and appalled the members of the Sanhedrin was Jesus' apparent claim—which he expressed through the striking imagery of the Hebrew Scriptures—that he himself was somehow divine. By making such a claim, Jesus had gone too far. He had taken the final step toward virtually guaranteeing that he would be executed.

The Trial Before Pilate

To carry out the death penalty against Jesus, the Jewish leadership needed the help of the Romans. However, the Roman procurator Pontius Pilate could not accept the charge of blasphemy as a sufficient reason for execution. Blasphemy was a religious offense, not a political one that in any way threatened the Roman state. The Jewish priests and elders then offered several alternative charges against Jesus: inciting the people to revolt against their Jewish leaders, opposing the payment of taxes to Caesar, and claiming to be the Messiah or a king (see Luke 23:2). Pilate was unmoved by those charges.

Pilate: Looking for a Way Out

Luke's Gospel includes a scene that is not contained in either of the other synoptic Gospels or in the Gospel of John: In front of Pilate, the Jewish leaders persist in their angry accusations about Jesus. Eventually Pilate learns that Jesus is a Galilean, and this gives Pilate an opening. The Jesus matter can thus be turned over to Herod Antipas, tetrarch of Galilee.

 Herod Antipas, son of Herod the Great, had been given authority over the region of Galilee after Herod the Great's death. The fact that Jesus was a Galilean, combined with the coincidence that Herod Antipas was in Jerusalem at the time the charges were brought against Jesus, gave Pilate one way out of his dilemma. He could avoid both the responsibility of condemning Jesus, whom he knew was innocent of anything deserving death, and the risk of further infuriating the Jews during the already emotionally intense time of Passover.

The problem was that Herod Antipas did not want to condemn Jesus either. Instead, according to Luke, "when Herod saw Jesus, he was very glad, for he had been wanting to see him for a long time, because he had heard about him and was hoping to see him perform some sign" (Luke 23:8, NRSV). When Jesus refused to respond to this expectation, an angry Herod Antipas sent him back to Pilate.

"I Am Innocent . . ."

As the angry cries of the Jewish leaders intensified, Pilate was left with only one more option. In accordance with the common practice of the Romans to release a Jewish prisoner during major religious feasts, he offered the Jewish leaders a choice: he could release either Jesus or another "notorious prisoner," who was named—perhaps coincidentally—Barabbas, meaning "son of the father."

The Jewish leaders were adamant about what they wanted—that Jesus be crucified. Pilate realized that the situation was hopeless. In a gesture described only in Matthew's Gospel, Pilate washed his hands in front of the crowds and said, "'I am innocent of this man's blood; see to it yourselves'" (27:24, NRSV). The "official" Roman charge against Jesus was that he had incited a revolt among the Jews.

Pilate's simple washing of his hands, of course, could not truly cleanse him of the guilt he was to share for the execution of Jesus. Some have tried to minimize his role in the trial, and there is a reasonable chance that the authors of the Gospels did so in an attempt to identify the Jewish leaders as the people chiefly responsible for Jesus' death. But the evidence is that Pilate, under pressure from an angry mob, condemned to death by crucifixion a man he knew to be innocent.

The Scourging and Crucifixion

In the Gospels—after all the building tensions and conflict, the touching and tragic encounter at Gethsemane, the hurried but complex inquiry and eventual trial—the execution of Jesus is described quickly and with near-frightening starkness.

"King of the Jews"

Before he was crucified, Jesus was first ridiculed by Roman soldiers for his claim to kingship, and he was given a soldier's scarlet cloak as a mocking tribute. A "crown" formed from a thorny plant was pressed onto his head. He was then the object of scourging, a beating often given prior to a crucifixion. During the scourging, Jesus was whipped with leather straps that had either bone or metal chips attached to them. Scourging was terribly brutal, many times leading to the death of prisoners as their flesh was literally torn from their body. Jesus survived.

Then Jesus was given a crossbeam to carry—not an entire cross, as so many paintings have depicted it. He was led to a small hill or mound called Golgotha, meaning "the Skull," perhaps because of its shape. There he was placed on his back, with his arms stretched across the crossbeam he had been carrying. Through his wrists he was nailed to the crossbeam, which was then lifted and attached to an upright beam that stood permanently in the ground. After being elevated, Jesus' body was tied to the cross with ropes around his arms, legs, and stomach, in order to keep his body from tearing free of the nails that held it. The cross also had a small "seat" built into the upright beam, on which the body could rest to ensure longer life and therefore greater suffering.

A small sign was nailed to the beam above Jesus' head, bearing the charge for which he was being executed. The sign read "King of the Jews." And he was left to hang there on the cross, between two crucified thieves, until he died.

A Spear in His Side

Crucifixion was the method of execution reserved for non-Roman citizens and slaves. (Capital punishment for Roman citizens was through the more "humane" method of beheading.) Sometimes a man would hang for a week or more on the cross before finally dying from bleeding, choking, inability to breathe, or even more hideous, being attacked by wild dogs during the nights. According to the Gospel accounts, Jesus died in six hours or less, surprising both Pilate and the guards.

According to John's Gospel, it was against the Jewish religious laws to have a body on a cross during the Sabbath, so the Jews asked that the legs of the three crucified men be broken to hasten death. (If a crucified man's legs were broken, he could not hold himself up to breathe.) But by the time the soldiers approached Jesus, he had already died.

Only John's account mentions that a soldier then pierced Jesus' side with a spear to guarantee his death before the Sabbath observance (John 19:31–37). Out of this wound, according to John, flowed blood and water. For John, water was a symbol of the Spirit. By adding this detail he may have intended to show that Jesus' death was the source of a great "outpouring" of the Spirit. Some ancient church theologians suggested that the blood and the water were symbols for the Christian sacraments of the Eucharist (blood) and baptism (water).

Jesus' Last Words

The Gospels provide differing versions of the words Jesus spoke on the cross before his death. Two of his statements, however, are particularly memorable:

"My God, my God . . .": According to both Mark and Matthew, Jesus uttered this statement, which is frequently recalled by believers and debated by scholars: "'My God, my God, why have you forsaken me?'" (Matt. 27:46, NRSV; see also Mark 15:34). Believers are touched by the statement because it reflects such deep loneliness and anxiety on the part of Jesus as he approaches his death. The debate of scholars centers on whether the words do in fact reflect a sense of deep despair. If the answer is yes, this in turn would seem to suggest that Jesus had a certain lack of faith in his Father's love for him.

Most scholars rightly point out that these words of Jesus are the opening line of Psalm 22. Faithful Jews traditionally memorized psalms in their entirety. By placing the first line of Psalm 22 on the lips of Jesus, the Evangelists were likely suggesting that the entire psalm was being recalled by Jesus. Scholars point out that although the psalm begins with a cry of distress and anguish, it ends with a strong statement of faith in Yahweh. While acknowledging the importance of this interpretation, we should not ignore the fact that the cry of Jesus on the cross reflects his undeniable humanity, which included moments of profound doubt and distress.

"Father, into your hands . . .": Of the three synoptic writers, only Luke specifically mentions Jesus' final words before he died. Matthew and Mark say that Jesus cried out in a loud voice and breathed his last (Matt. 27:50; Mark 15:37). John records Jesus' closing words in this way: "When Jesus had received the wine, he said, 'It is finished.' Then he bowed his head and gave up his spirit"; that is, he died (19:30, NRSV).

The words that Luke places on Jesus' lips, if not actually spoken by Jesus, no doubt reflect the attitude he carried with him to his death: "'Father, into your hands I commend my spirit'" (23:46, NRSV).

Understanding the Cross

Throughout the history of the church, the struggle to come to terms with Jesus' death has led to a wide variety of expressions, symbols, and theological interpretations. Certainly the cross has a profound and complex significance for Christians, one that may well be too great for words.

Common Expressions

Jesus' death has been referred to as a "sacrifice," perhaps reflecting the Passover theme mentioned earlier. It is said that Jesus "died for our sins," that he "conquered death," that he "gave his life as a ransom for many." It would be easy but dangerous to settle on any one expression to capture the complex meaning of the cross. In doing so, we would risk seriously misinterpreting the cross's meaning. Let's look at these common expressions to see what they can tell us about that meaning.

Jesus Died for Our Sins

Perhaps the most popular statement about the death of Jesus—the cross—is, "He died for our sins." This statement is certainly appropriate and accurate when suggesting that Jesus' death was a result of the sinfulness of humanity. Jesus' death, as the ultimate expression of God's love for humanity, also saves people from the devastating effects of sin, in that God made the Son of God one with us, even in our sinfulness, so that in his death we might be reconciled with God.

Unfortunately, when taken too far, this wording is confusing for many of us. It can convey an image of God that is far removed from the one Jesus revealed to the world. Such a statement can give a sense, for instance, that Jesus had to die in our place in order to satisfy an angry God who was demanding a "pound of flesh" in payment for past offenses. This image of God runs directly contrary to Jesus' message—that God is a totally loving and forgiving Father.

Jesus Conquered Death

Jesus' death can also be understood as a decisive confrontation between good and evil, between the forces of life and the forces of death. As the next chapter in this handbook will show, what at first appears to be the death of both Jesus and his Dream of the Kingdom of God is eventually recognized as a total victory by God in Jesus' Resurrection. In that sense we can say, "Jesus conquered death."

Jesus Gave His Life as a Ransom for Many

Another insight into the meaning of Jesus' death can be found in Mark 10:45, where Jesus states that "'the Son of Man came not to be served but to serve, and to give his life [as] a ransom for many'" (NRSV). When properly understood, this can be a helpful expression for us.

In the Roman world, a ransom was the price paid to release a slave, and it was often paid by someone other than the slave. The idea of ransom can help us understand the cross if we recognize ourselves as being in slavery to sin and Jesus' ransoming us from sin by his death—an incredibly freeing act of love that knows no limits.

Only in Light of the Resurrection

At this point in the discussion, we are, in a sense, trying to understand the cross too soon. We cannot completely understand the execution of Jesus until we understand what followed it—Jesus' being raised from the dead by his Father.

None of the Gospels ends with Jesus' Passion and death on the cross. Rather, we see Jesus' total trust in God at the moment of his death—"Father, into your hands I commend my spirit." That trust in God is then proven to be well founded in light of the Resurrection. Only through the Resurrection can we see the ultimate message of the cross: God loves all people unconditionally. As the Evangelist John would say years after Jesus' death:

> Whoever does not love does not know God, for God is love. God's love was revealed among us in this way: God sent his only Son into the world so that we might live through him. In this is love, not that we loved God but that he loved us and sent his Son to be the atoning sacrifice for our sins. Beloved, since God loved us so much, we also ought to love one another. (1 John 4:8–11, NRSV)

7

The Resurrection and Ascension:
Jesus Is Alive and Present

The final two sessions of the formation period are pivotal sessions in *Confirmed in a Faithful Community* in three ways:

1. The sessions deal with the theologically central and critical issues of Jesus' Resurrection, Pentecost, and the birth of the church.

2. These two sessions offer a transition in the process of preparation in terms of content— from a focus on Jesus and his message to one on the church and its mission.

3. These sessions are programmatically pivotal in that they move us from somewhat lengthy and remote preparation for confirmation to the more intense and immediate preparation for celebration of the sacrament itself in the period of reflection.

   This chapter provides the theological background needed for formation session 7, "The Resurrection of Jesus: God Is Victorious!" The intent here is to treat this admittedly challenging theological material in a style that is clear and accessible— for both the candidates and the catechists! Careful reflection on this material will pay real dividends in preparing you to lead the candidates through this important phase of their preparation for confirmation.

The Resurrection as an Event

The Gospels themselves—indeed, Christianity as a recognized religion—would not even exist were it not for what happened *after* the death of Jesus. The last days of Jesus' earthly life—his arrest, trial, and death by crucifixion—have been recalled and passed on for some two thousand years only because they were followed by an event that gave them meaning. That event, of course, was the Resurrection, Jesus' being raised from the dead by God, his Father, on Easter.

Curiously, the Gospel accounts of the Resurrection of Jesus are brief compared with those of the final days of Jesus' life. The accounts of the event found in the Gospels are surprisingly straightforward, offer little detail, and make no attempt to further explain what happened. Many of us might like to ask the Evangelists a few of the following questions:

- What did Jesus look like when he was raised from the dead by God?
- Did anyone actually see Jesus come out of the tomb?
- If no one saw him, how do we know that he was really raised? Maybe somebody just stole the body to make people *think* he was raised.
- How can people today be expected to believe something so incredible, something that is almost unbelievable?

All of these are good, reasonable questions. This chapter will attempt to provide some satisfying answers.

What Happened?

Each Gospel tells of the burial and Resurrection of Jesus and some of his appearances to his disciples and others after the Resurrection (see Matt. 27:62–66; 28:1–20; Mark 15:42–47; 16:1–20; Luke 23:50–56; 24:1–53; and John 19:38–42; 20:1–31; 21:1–25). Despite the many differences between these accounts, we can arrive at a basic sense of what occurred that remarkable Sunday morning long ago.

Jesus Was Buried in a Tomb

All four Gospel accounts agree that after Jesus died, his body was claimed by a wealthy disciple of Jesus named Joseph of Arimathea. Joseph had asked Pilate for the right to take the body and give it a decent burial. He took the body, wrapped it in a burial cloth called a shroud, and laid it in a tomb hewn out of stone. (The full preparation of the body for burial according to Jewish custom had to wait until after the Sabbath, which was already beginning on the evening of the Friday Jesus died.) A large, round, flat stone was then rolled into place at the entrance of the tomb. Matthew's Gospel states that Pontius Pilate assigned Roman soldiers to guard the tomb, to prevent Jesus' disciples from stealing the body. The Jewish leaders were concerned that the disciples would steal the body and then claim that Jesus had risen from the dead as he had predicted he would.

Other Common Points in the Gospel Accounts

After describing Jesus' burial, each Evangelist offers his own version of what happened. However, the accounts do have these points in common:

- Various people go to the tomb and discover that the body of Jesus is no longer there.
- The people who go to the tomb find out—either on their own (in John's Gospel) or through one or more messengers of God (in the synoptic Gospels)—that Jesus is no longer dead but alive, and that he will reveal himself to them again soon.
- The initial reactions of the witnesses are, quite naturally, shock and then fear. But soon they experience Jesus among them in such striking ways that there can be no doubt it is he—alive again, and yet somehow very different from when he walked among them before his death. Jesus has risen, and everything he claimed is proved true by this fact.

Focusing on the Larger Picture

Beyond the common points listed above, a number of differences in the Gospel accounts of the Resurrection are easily recognized with just a quick reading of those accounts. However, remember this basic lesson about the Gospels: The small details in the accounts are not significant or essential to what is being revealed through them. The truths expressed in and through the accounts far surpass any inconsistency that might be apparent in them.

Evidence of the Resurrection as an Event

Saint Paul, in his first letter to the Corinthians, states, "If Christ has not been raised, then empty . . . is our preaching; empty, too, your faith" (15:14, NAB). No factor in Christian faith is more central, more important, more critical, to our understanding of the Christ of Faith than the Resurrection. Ultimately, recognizing the Risen Christ is a matter of faith. Yet considerable historical evidence supports the Christian conviction of the Resurrection of Jesus by his Father.

A Consistent Belief in the Early Church

The Resurrection was a consistent belief in the early church. The letters of Saint Paul, sermons contained in the Acts of the Apostles, and all four Gospels mention it. In Acts, we see that experiencing the Risen Jesus was even considered a key qualification for being accepted as one of the Apostles (Acts 1:15–22).

The Empty Tomb

The empty tomb also testifies to the reality of the Resurrection. All accounts of the Resurrection agree that the tomb was empty on the morning that the women went to prepare Jesus' body for burial. Surely the Romans would have produced Jesus' corpse if they could have found it. Publicly displaying his dead body would have immediately destroyed any stories of his Resurrection that might have been falsely created by his disciples.

But one might ask, Could the disciples have somehow stolen the corpse and then either hidden or destroyed it? The problem with this proposition is that many of the disciples would eventually choose to die as martyrs rather than deny their faith in a resurrected Jesus. Would they have freely died for a hoax, knowing that Jesus had not really risen?

Moreover, the Gospels identify women as major witnesses to the empty tomb. In the ancient Jewish society, women were not accepted as legal witnesses. Therefore, an author seeking to convince an audience of something untrue would never have chosen women as primary witnesses; they were not perceived as credible.

Jesus' Post-Resurrection Appearances

Though no one actually witnessed the Resurrection itself, many claimed to have experienced the Risen Jesus later. Though the Gospels disagree on who saw him where and when and under what circumstances, the appearances do follow a common pattern:

* Everyone to whom Jesus appears is downcast, distressed, clearly convinced that he is dead.
* Jesus then takes the initiative and reveals himself to them, usually greeting them with the statement that they should be unafraid and at peace.
* Finally, Jesus often gives a command, such as "'Go therefore and make disciples of all nations'" (Matt. 28:19, NRSV) or "'Go into all the world and proclaim the good news to the whole creation'" (Mark 16:15, NRSV). The knowledge of Jesus Risen is not to be kept secret, as a private revelation. Those who know him are clearly called to share that knowledge with others.

Note how the empty tomb and the apparitions of Jesus are consistent with, and thus firm up and solidify, each other. Without the empty tomb, the appearances of Jesus could be regarded as hallucinations, as the fantasies of depressed people. Without the appearances, the empty tomb could be considered a trick.

A Transformed Community

A final piece of evidence can be offered to support the reality of Jesus' Resurrection: a thoroughly shattered band of Jesus' followers was transformed into a community of courageous witnesses after the Resurrection. This may be the most important evidence of all. The total conviction with which the disciples proclaimed the Risen Jesus as a sign of joy and hope is undeniable. After all, only such a conviction—and the commitment to share the faith motivated by that conviction—can explain the beginning of the church.

Proclamations of Faith

The Gospel accounts of the Resurrection, we must always remember, are not attempts to record in historical detail what occurred the day we call Easter. This does not mean that the Resurrection did not happen. On the contrary, the Risen Jesus is the most consistently proclaimed reality in the entire Christian Testament. And the Resurrection is the most pivotal event proclaimed by the Gospels. Only if God actually raised Jesus from the dead is the truth of both Jesus and his message confirmed. Only then is the Gospel proclamation truly Good News, not a lie, a hoax, or a fantasy to be rejected.

As proclamations of faith rather than historical documents, the Gospel accounts and their inconsistent details should not be a stumbling block to believing in Jesus' Resurrection. The Resurrection simply was not a historical event in the usual sense. The death of Jesus was historical in that even nonbelievers would have been able to see Jesus crucified. But only people of faith experienced Jesus after his Resurrection, and even they sometimes had great difficulty and hesitation. The Risen Jesus could not have been scientifically proven to exist. The Resurrection, in other words, goes beyond history as we know it.

What Was the Risen Jesus Like?

What did the Risen Jesus look like? Exactly how did the disciples experience him? What seems certain yet mysterious in the Gospel accounts is that Jesus was truly transformed through the Resurrection. He was experiencing an utterly new kind of existence. The Risen Jesus was not a person who had been asleep and then suddenly awakened, nor was he a corpse that had somehow come back to life. He was the same Jesus and yet completely different.

Resurrected life is not merely a continuation, after death, of the kind of earthly life we experience. It is, rather, an entirely new way of living, a new relationship in and with God, something completely beyond our imagination. How can we explain this kind of life? The simple answer is, we can't! Nonbelievers have suggested that the authors of the Christian Testament imagined or intentionally created a vision of resurrected life. But it would seem that the Gospel evidence supporting the Resurrection of Jesus is too complex and too thorough to have been created by any one author, let alone several authors working independently of one another.

The Resurrection and Christian Faith

Let's take a closer look at why the Resurrection is of critical importance to Christian faith.

Affirmation of the Truth of Jesus' Teachings

Of most significance to Christian faith is the fact that the Resurrection demonstrates the truth of Jesus' claims and teachings about God.

- In his claim about God's unconditional love for each of us, Jesus spoke the truth.
- In his promise that we can find fulfillment in loving God and others, Jesus spoke the truth.
- In his rejection of empty religious ritual and his commitment to a prayerful and personal relationship with God, Jesus spoke the truth.
- In his conviction that forgiveness of one another will always be more life-giving and enriching than revenge, Jesus spoke the truth.
- In his call for respect and special affection for the outcasts of society, Jesus spoke the truth.
- In his teaching that rich people must share with poor people, Jesus spoke the truth.
- In his absolute refusal to accept anything that would separate people from one another—social status, sexual or racial discrimination, economic standing, political affiliation, even religious beliefs—Jesus spoke the truth.

All of this is affirmed by the Resurrection.

Jesus Recognized as the Messiah

The Resurrection demonstrates as well that Jesus was and is forever the Messiah, the Christ, not just a great, good man with a marvelous but unrealistic Dream.

Many people want to give a halfhearted, incomplete assent to Jesus and his message. They are willing to admit that he was a special person, perhaps the greatest in history, and certainly one worth imitating. But the Messiah, the Lord, the Christ? That is going too far, they say.

The Resurrection of Jesus, together with the church's constant commitment to belief in the Resurrection as the central characteristic of Christian faith, makes a conditional acceptance of Jesus, as merely an extraordinary human being, an unacceptable response for Christians. As stated earlier in this book, Jesus had to be one of three things: a lunatic, a con artist, or exactly who he professed to be. The Resurrection points in favor of the last option: Jesus was and is the One sent by God to redeem the world.

Life in Christ

For Christians, the Resurrection of Jesus completely transforms the understanding of all human life. Because of the Resurrection, Christians know that happiness and fullness of life are not accomplished merely through rigid religious practices or through some new self-improvement program. Rather, happiness and fullness of life come from a new "center," a new "life force," a new source of power. That new source of power is nothing less than God, the God that is revealed in and through Jesus Christ. "'I live now not with my own life,'" said Saint Paul, "'but with the life of Christ who lives in me'" (Gal. 2:20, JB).

From Death to New Life: The Paschal Mystery

A New Passover

The Evangelist John linked the death of Jesus with the killing of the paschal lambs, which were slaughtered as part of the Passover celebration. John's Gospel refers to Jesus as the "new paschal lamb," "the lamb of God, who takes away the sins of the world." The church's phrase *paschal mystery* builds on this theme and refers to the profound meaning that the death and Resurrection of Jesus can hold for many aspects of human life.

Paschal mystery refers first and foremost to the ways Jesus' death and Resurrection constitute a "new Passover" for history and for those who believe in Jesus. The Christian Testament speaks of Jesus' death and Resurrection as bringing about redemption. That is, Jesus' death and Resurrection save all humanity from death and the powers of sin. As discussed earlier, Christians speak of this salvation in many ways—by saying, for example, that Jesus died for our sins, that he gave his life as a ransom for many.

The Paschal Mystery in Everyday Life

To understand the redemptive meaning of the paschal mystery, Christians point to the recurring theme of dying and rising found in everyday experiences.

In nature: Much of nature reflects a repeating cycle of death and rebirth. Reflect, for example, on the plant life that thrives in your yard or in parks near where you live. Many plants flourish during the summer, wilt and "die" in the fall and winter, only to bloom again each spring. Animals are born, grow to maturity, generate new life, and then die, only to decay and provide nourishment for new life. People too, of course, reflect this pattern on the level of biology.

In pain experiences: The redemptive meaning of the paschal mystery can be witnessed in personal ways as well as in the cycle of nature. Christians believe, for example, that much of the pain encountered in life—whether physical, emotional, intellectual, or spiritual—can serve as an invitation to and opportunity for new growth, when seen with the eyes of faith. When a friend is suffering, an act of love on our part can bring new life to our friend and to ourselves. When a person hurts us through an unkind word or careless action, a gesture of forgiveness from us can renew the relationship and bring it to new depth.

This is not to say that pain and suffering should be sought. Enough of it comes inevitably with life. Through the Resurrection, God lets us know that ultimately, pain and suffering are not what life is about. When responded to with faith, hope, and especially love, pain and suffering can provide the ground from which new life springs. Then the paschal mystery is again made real.

From death to resurrection and new life—the paschal mystery seems to permeate all of life for those with "the eyes to see and ears to hear" (see Mark 8:18, NRSV). Perhaps only when the paschal mystery is lived out in the actions and attitudes of daily life can the full meaning of Jesus' death and Resurrection make sense for the Christian.

The Risen Jesus

The appearances of the Risen Jesus to various people following the Resurrection give us fascinating insights into the nature of resurrected life. The appearances also offer us an important understanding of the nature of Jesus' presence in the world today.

An Extraordinary God Is Revealed in Ordinary Ways

The Gospels do not record that blazing trumpets, magical signs, or roaring crowds accompanied the Risen Jesus' appearances. On the contrary, he appeared simply and humanly. Mary Magdalene at first thought that Jesus was a simple gardener. Yet when he called her name, she suddenly recognized him. In a beautiful scene recorded in Luke's Gospel (24:13–35), Jesus took a long walk with two terrified and hopeless disciples who were totally shattered by the Crucifixion. Jesus slowly revealed to them the meaning of the events, and in the simple gesture of breaking bread together, they finally recognized him as their Lord and Master. Jesus also appeared to some totally shocked and frightened disciples who felt at first that they were seeing a ghost. He told them that they had nothing to fear, then asked simply if they had anything to eat. Jesus shared a simple breakfast of fish by a lakeshore with Peter and others.

In all these appearances the people were shattered by what had happened in the Crucifixion, were totally unprepared for the Resurrection, and were stunned by the one who was now present among them. In all cases Jesus brought overwhelming peace and joy.

The Resurrected Jesus: Present in a New Way

Some researchers have proposed the idea that Jesus actually survived the Crucifixion and that the later appearances were simply made when he recovered. However, Jesus' appearances began within days of the Crucifixion, and the brutal tortures that Jesus suffered from his scourging and execution would normally have required lengthy recovery.

Jesus' resurrected body, admittedly, was not his physical body simply recovered to health. Jesus had changed. In many of his appearances Jesus was not easily recognized. Only people with faith or with at least an openness to faith recognized him. Jesus had entered into an entirely new form of existence. He appeared and then suddenly disappeared. Closed doors could not keep him out. He was still definitely Jesus, but at the same time, he was considerably different from the Jesus who had walked among the people for so many years.

The appearances offer us an important insight because they are transitional moments. That is, the appearances reveal the change from Jesus' earthly presence two thousand years ago to his presence as we experience it today. Jesus is no longer present among us in a physical way—that is, we can no longer see him with our eyes or hear him with our ears or touch him with our hands. Nevertheless, Jesus is truly present among us. As he promised, Jesus is present through his Spirit, a Spirit who continually brings back to our mind all that Jesus taught us and gives us the courage and insight to live out that message.

The appearances offer another, related insight about Jesus' risen life: present through his Spirit in our midst, Jesus can only be recognized with eyes of faith. Even the disciples who experienced his appearances had to have faith. The wonderfully touching story of Doubting Thomas illustrates this point:

> Thomas, called the Twin, who was one of the Twelve, was not with them when Jesus came. So the other disciples said to him, "We have seen the Lord," but he answered, "Unless I can see the holes that the nails made in his hands and can put my finger into the holes they made, and unless I can put my hand into his side, I refuse to believe." Eight days later the disciples were in the house again and Thomas was with them. The doors were closed, but Jesus came in and stood among them. "Peace be with you," he said. Then he spoke to Thomas, "Put your finger here; look, here are my hands. Give me your hand; put it into my side. Do not be unbelieving any more but believe." Thomas replied, "My Lord and my God!" Jesus said to him:
> "You believe because you can see me.
> Blessed are those who have not seen and yet believe."
> (John 20:24–29, NJB)

To be fair to Thomas, we should remember that earlier he had indicated his willingness to die with Jesus (John 11:16).

The greatly encouraging fact here is that even eyewitnesses sometimes had difficulty recognizing and accepting Jesus. Today we often seem to think that if only we could see him, if only Jesus appeared directly to us, if only we could walk with him, touch him, hear his voice, then faith would follow. The appearances demonstrate that faith was required even of those who were present at those marvelous moments, that only in faith were they able to recognize Jesus in their midst. We too can recognize him clearly through the eyes of faith.

The Ascension of Jesus

What happened to Jesus after his Resurrection and his appearances to the disciples and others? Our immediate inclination is to respond that he "went to heaven." But where and what is heaven? And how did he get from here to there? These are perhaps obvious questions, but they have anything but obvious answers.

What the Scriptures Tell Us

Numerous parts of the Christian Testament refer to Jesus' presence with the Father "in heaven." For example, Jesus is said to be "seated at the right hand of God." However, specific references to the Ascension of Jesus into the presence of his Father are fewer in number.

- A specific description of the Ascension of Jesus as a historical event is made only in Luke's Gospel and in the second part of Luke's work, which is called the Acts of the Apostles.
- Neither Matthew's Gospel nor John's Gospel mentions the Ascension at all, and the brief mention of the event in Mark 16:19 may have been added to Mark's original Gospel.
- Only two brief references to the Ascension can be found in all the Epistles (1 Tim. 3:16; 1 Pet. 3:22).

In his Gospel account of the Ascension, Luke says, "[Jesus] led them out as far as Bethany, and, lifting up his hands, he blessed them. While he was blessing them, he withdrew from them and was carried up into heaven" (24:50–51, NRSV).

According to the account given in Acts, Jesus promised his disciples, "'You will receive power when the Holy Spirit has come upon you'" (1:8, NRSV).

When he had said this, as they were watching, he was lifted up, and a cloud took him out of their sight. While he was going and they were gazing up toward heaven, suddenly two men in white robes stood by them. [The men in robes] said, "Men of Galilee, why do you stand looking up toward heaven? This Jesus, who has been taken up from you into heaven, will come in the same way as you saw him go into heaven." (1:9–11, NRSV)

An Event Beyond Human Comprehension

As was true of the earlier Gospel accounts, contradictions and differences are evident in the various scriptural references to the Ascension. These contradictions and differences are understandable, given the fact that the writers of the Christian story were dealing with an event beyond human comprehension. A happening of this magnitude stretches our ability to express it within the limits of language.

A Problem of Space and Time

We, as humans, cannot escape images of space and time in our speaking, writing, and even thinking. For example, we automatically think of heaven as a place "up there." This notion may have been inherited from the people of Jesus' day, who had a simplistic view of the universe.

The ancient Jews viewed the universe as consisting of several "layers": the earth itself; the firmament above it, which included the sky and the stars; and the abyss, which lay beneath the earth. The people imagined the realm or world of God as existing beyond the sky and the waters above the sky. It was natural for the scriptural authors, therefore, to express their recognition of Jesus as the Risen Messiah who transcends time and space, through use of images of time and space, stating that Jesus was "lifted into the heavens" at a particular time and place.

In spite of our limited understanding of Jesus' Ascension, we can get a handle on the meaning the scriptural authors intended to express through their description of this event.

Right Here, Right Now

The main lesson that the scriptural authors wished to teach by describing the Ascension was this: Following his Resurrection, Jesus passed totally into the presence of God and in doing so, he moved beyond the limits of space and time. What this actually means—strangely enough—is precisely the opposite of what we often assume it means. When we speak of the Risen Jesus as "going to his Father," we naturally think in terms of Jesus' being removed from our earthly realm, of his being separated from us. But when we reflect upon where God is (in light of Jesus' teachings about his Father), we realize that it is not right to speak and think of God as "out there" somewhere. The entire message of Jesus hinges on precisely the opposite realization—that the Kingdom of God is among us, that God is not "out there" but rather "right here."

Even small children acknowledge God as "being everywhere." But think of what this implies: If God is totally present, if God is right here and right now, then by "going to the Father," Jesus was actually becoming more truly present to us than he could possibly have been as he walked the roads of Palestine! Now free of the limitations of space and time that bind humans, Jesus can be totally with us. He is no longer tied down to one place at one time, talking about one thing to one particular group of people—as was true two thousand years ago. Rather, he is free to be everywhere, with everyone, for all time, loving and caring and calling us to his Father. This is the marvelous reality of the Good News!

The introduction to this chapter noted the pivotal nature of formation sessions 7 and 8 and the related material in this handbook. In the next chapter, we explore *the* pivotal theme in *Confirmed in a Faithful Community* as we reflect on a biblical event, following Jesus' Resurrection and Ascension, that is closely connected with the sacrament of confirmation—Pentecost, an event many refer to as "the birthday of the church."

8

Pentecost:
Gift of the Spirit and
Birth of the Church

Formation session 8, "Pentecost: Gift of the Spirit and Birth of the Church," brings the discussion of Jesus and his Gospel proclamation of the Reign of God to a close and then redirects the primary focus of *Confirmed in a Faithful Community* to the church and the meaning of membership in it. The pivotal biblical event related to this transition is, of course, Pentecost and its effects among the early community of believers. That event and its significance are the focus of this chapter.

Pentecost:
The Gift of the Holy Spirit

Shortly after describing the Ascension of Jesus, Luke describes another marvelous event that occurred as the Apostles gathered together in a room on the annual Jewish feast of Pentecost. This particular celebration of the feast of Pentecost occurred fifty days after Easter, that is, after the Resurrection of Jesus. Luke gives the following account:

> When Pentecost day came round, they had all met together, when suddenly there came from heaven a sound as of a violent wind which filled the entire house in which they were sitting; and there appeared to them tongues as of fire; these separated and came to rest on the head of each of them. They were all filled with the Holy Spirit and began to speak different languages as the Spirit gave them power to express themselves.
>
> Now there were devout men living in Jerusalem from every nation under heaven, and at this sound they all assembled, and each one was bewildered to hear these men speaking his own language. They were amazed and astonished. "Surely," they said, "all these men speaking are Galileans? How does it happen that each of us hears them in his own native language? . . . We hear them preaching in our own language about the marvels of God." Everyone was amazed and perplexed; they asked one another what it all meant. Some, however, laughed it off. "They have been drinking too much new wine," they said. (Acts 2:1–13, NJB)

Christians refer to this wondrous event as Pentecost.

Jesus Fully Present in His Spirit

Jesus had promised his followers that he would send his Spirit—also referred to as the Helper, Comforter, and Advocate. His Spirit would remain with them and help them lead the life to which he was calling them. As Jesus says in John's Gospel:

"Still, I am telling you the truth:
it is for your own good that I am going,
because unless I go,
the Paraclete [Advocate] will not come to you;
but if I go,
I will send him to you."

(16:7, NJB)

Jesus' bodily presence, as experienced by the Apostles, was to be replaced by the presence of the Spirit, and through the Spirit, Jesus would be profoundly and truly present.

The Spirit in Jewish History

Belief in the Spirit did not begin with Jesus. As a devout Jew, Jesus was very conscious of a long history of waiting for the Spirit of God to be sent by Yahweh to the Jews. The Hebrew Scriptures refer to the Spirit many times, mentioning the activity of the Spirit in creation, in the history of the Jewish people, and in a special way in the life and words of the great prophets. The dream of the Jewish people was that the Spirit would someday dwell in each of them. Immediately following the Pentecost event, the Acts of the Apostles shows Peter trying to explain the incredible event by recalling the prophecy of the prophet Joel:

In the last days—the Lord declares—
I shall pour out my Spirit on all humanity.
Your sons and daughters shall prophesy,
your young people shall see visions,
your old people dream dreams.
Even on the slaves, men and women,
shall I pour out my Spirit.
I will show portents in the sky above
and signs on earth below.
The sun will be turned into darkness
and the moon into blood
before the day of the Lord comes,
that great and terrible Day.
And all who call on the name of the Lord will be saved.

(Acts 2:17–21, NJB)

This strong imagery is typical of the preaching style of the prophets and indeed of much of the Scriptures. Apparently the biblical authors wished to speak of realities that were simply too great to be conveyed through ordinary language. For example, the Hebrew word for *spirit* also means "breath" or "breath of wind." Water and fire are also used as scriptural images for the Spirit of God. We must be sensitive to this use of vivid language if we are to fully understand the true intent of the Scriptures.

A New Covenant Revealed

Something special happened to the Apostles on Pentecost. Many other examples of the outpouring of the Spirit occurred in the days of the early church, but this one event on the feast day of the Sinai Covenant was particularly significant. Christians believe that on this day God established an entirely new covenant with people. In the minds of Christians, this covenant was promised in the Hebrew Scriptures. For instance, the prophet Ezekiel had said, "I shall give you a new heart, and put a new spirit in you; I shall remove the heart of stone from your bodies and give you a heart of flesh instead" (Ezek. 36:26, NJB). The prophet Jeremiah had spoken in a similar way:

> I shall make a new covenant with the House of Israel . . . but not like the covenant I made with their ancestors the day I took them by the hand to bring them out of Egypt. . . . Within them I shall plant my Law, writing it on their hearts. Then I shall be their God and they will be my people. (Jer. 31:31–33, NJB)

This new covenant between God and all people was established through the life, death, and Resurrection of Jesus and continues through the presence of the Spirit.

The Strange Events Surrounding Pentecost

The description of Pentecost is filled with marvelous imagery. Did all this actually happen? Did tongues of fire truly appear, did strong winds blow, did people speak in a marvelous language that all could understand? We simply do not know for sure. Regarding the marvelous language, the biblical writer may be reminding us of the story of the Tower of Babel in the Book of Genesis. In that story, human languages were multiplied and communication destroyed. On Pentecost, by contrast, the Spirit brought unity and understanding.

What we can be certain of is that the Apostles shared an incredibly intense experience, an experience that changed them radically and permanently. The immediate result of the presence of the Spirit was unbridled joy, so much so that bystanders thought the Apostles must be drunk. Peter quickly reminded them that it was only 9 o'clock in the morning (Acts 2:15).

As with the Resurrection and the appearances of Jesus, we must be careful not to lose sight of the meaning of Pentecost in our concern about the marvel-filled details of Luke's account. If we concentrate too much on the descriptive images, we may be led to believe that the event is completely foreign to our experience, and consequently not significant.

Some people might, in fact, experience Jesus' presence in spectacular and astounding ways. In his appearances, however, Jesus revealed that he was also encountered in the everyday experiences of life—for example, in the sharing of a meal, in greeting a friend, or while engaging in a conversation. Similarly, we can encounter Jesus' Spirit in the common events of our life. Saint Paul's letter to the Galatians describes the effects of the Spirit's presence as love, joy, peace, patience, goodness, among other qualities (5:22–23). In other words, the Spirit is revealed most effectively and most commonly in lives filled with these simple qualities, not with the kind of special effects that we find in Hollywood films.

The Seven Gifts of the Holy Spirit

The Bible offers another insight into the workings of the Spirit—an insight drawn from a passage from the Hebrew Scriptures:

> A shoot will spring from the stock of Jesse,
> a new shoot will grow from his roots.
> On him will rest the spirit of Yahweh,
> the spirit of wisdom and insight,
> the spirit of counsel and power,
> the spirit of knowledge and fear of Yahweh.
>
> (Isa. 11: 1–3, NJB)

Christians think that this passage refers to Jesus, who descended from the line of King David, Jesse's son. Christians understand that Jesus fully possessed the qualities described in Galatians and that believers are now invited to share in them through the power of the Spirit. The seven gifts of the Holy Spirit include wisdom, understanding, right judgment, knowledge, courage, love, and reverence. These gifts are often referred to in the theology and celebration of confirmation. In the Rite of Confirmation, the bishop mentions them as the qualities that characterize Christians' daily lives.

Pentecost: The Birth of the Church

For many people the word *church* refers to the building in which Christians worship or, less often, to those who take particular leadership in the church—bishops, the pope, and so on. The fact is that the church is most clearly understood in light of Pentecost. The church is, simply yet profoundly, *the gathering of those people who profess faith in the Risen Jesus and his message and who, through the power of the Spirit, live their lives in loving service to all people.* Traditionally, Christians claim that the church began with the experience of a chosen few in that small room on the feast of Pentecost nearly two thousand years ago. What occurred to those few has been repeated again and again throughout history—with less drama and fewer wondrous displays, but just as truly.

From the time of Jesus' death and Resurrection until today, people have been touched by his Spirit, and so they have gathered in communities of faith. In and through these communities, believers constantly grow in their understanding of Jesus' message. They also support one another as they try to live out in their daily life the demands of their faith. These believers pray together, share their concerns and their gifts, and constantly call to mind and celebrate the powerful presence of the Lord in their midst. In so doing, the church stands as a herald of the Kingdom of God, a messenger to the larger world of the Reign of God that was announced by Jesus. We turn now to a more thorough discussion of this very special community of Christian believers that we call the church.

Understanding the Church

After his description of the presence of Jesus' Spirit on Pentecost and of Saint Peter's address to the crowds that witnessed that event, Luke continues his writing in the Acts of the Apostles with the following description of the earliest days in the church:

[The people were convinced by Peter's arguments.] They accepted what he said and were baptised. That very day about three thousand were added to their number.

These remained faithful to the teaching of the apostles, to the brotherhood, to the breaking of bread and to the prayers.

And everyone was filled with awe; the apostles worked many signs and miracles.

And all who shared the faith owned everything in common; they sold their goods and possessions and distributed the proceeds among themselves according to what each one needed.

Each day, with one heart, they regularly went to the Temple but met in their houses for the breaking of bread; they shared their food gladly and generously; they praised God and were looked up to by everyone. Day by day the Lord added to their community those destined to be saved. (Acts 2:41–47, NJB)

To Christians today this scriptural passage contains some familiar ideas and actions. For example:

- The notion of gathering for prayer is a common experience for Christians today, as is the joining for the "breaking of bread"— which we now call Eucharist or Mass.
- This passage also describes a sense of tremendous generosity, a willingness to share one's goods. Many Christians have witnessed similar generosity in weekly offertory collections at Mass, in the gathering of food and clothing for poor people; in the building of churches, hospitals, and schools; and in many other uplifting experiences in the church today.
- The sense of shared purpose and vision in Luke's description is so much a part of the experience of the church that at times its members take that sense for granted. Many practicing Catholics are struck by their Catholic identity, for instance, only when experiencing the religious expressions of other Christian denominations or of other faiths.

Reading the description of the early church in Acts, we might also feel that we are eavesdropping at someone else's party. We are witnessing the activities of an entirely new religious movement that may seem foreign to our experience of the church. The members of that early Christian community, for example, not only celebrated their common faith but also owned everything in common. Likewise they went to homes, not to churches, to worship. Finally, that first community grew at a rapid rate, with new members joining day by day.

The early church, which gathered immediately after Pentecost to proclaim and celebrate the life, death, and Resurrection of Jesus, is the bedrock upon which the contemporary church is founded. In fact, the early church and the modern church are one and the same: today's church is that same Christian community with some two thousand years of history behind it. Yet much has happened to the church during those many years.

The Present Is Based on the Past

Christians are bearers of a message that is almost literally out of this world. Yet they are attempting to live out that message *in* this world. Because the church is a community of people, it is affected directly by the world—that is, by historical events, by cultural influences, by social movements, and by contact with new ideas and new philosophies. The constant challenge to the church has been to maintain its roots while growing new shoots. In other words, the church, while striving to remain true to Jesus' message, also struggles to explain that message to new and changing cultures.

In trying to achieve these twin goals—of fidelity and flexibility—the church has acted like the very human community that it is. That is to say, the church, in acts of courage, dignity, creativity, and loving service, has demonstrated throughout its history the presence of God's grace. Yet the church has also demonstrated occasional small-mindedness, selfishness, brutality, and the constant presence of sin.

A final comment by way of introduction to our discussion of the church: Catholics are often inclined to think of Catholic Christianity as *the* church and to think of other Christian denominations as *other* churches. The reality is that *the* church includes all those who profess faith in Jesus Christ and are committed to seeking the

Kingdom of God by living out their faith in loving service. The Catholic church, however, believes that the fullness of Christ's saving revelation and the fullness of the means for salvation are present in the Catholic church, though shared by other Christian churches in varying degrees.

The major point here is that, in general, Christians of various traditions are much more alike than they are different from one another. Roman Catholics have been leaders in the effort to reunite Christian churches, at least to the point that all churches can respect one another. In discussions of the church in *Confirmed in a Faithful Community,* the term *the church* means the entire Christian church, not only Catholicism. In those cases when the program focuses on religious expressions that are uniquely Catholic—for example, the seven Catholic sacraments or the pope—the terms *Catholic Christianity* or the *Catholic church* are used. The term *Protestant* is used to refer to non-Catholic Christian churches stemming from the Protestant revolution of the seventeenth century.

The Church as a People of Faith

The previous section on Pentecost offered a working definition of the church: The church is the gathering of those people who profess faith in the Risen Jesus and his message and who, through the power of the Holy Spirit, live their lives in loving service to all people. Let's take a closer look at this definition.

A gathering of people: By nature we are communal. That is, we gather in communities for self-preservation, for the sharing of goods and services, and for many other human needs. The experience of God also seems to be communal: as individual persons we discover God through our contact with other people, through our human relationships, and most directly, through our contact with formal communities of believers. Once God is discovered by individuals, the desire to share that discovery with others is natural, almost necessary. So that is one facet of the church—people coming together to share a common experience.

A people professing faith in Jesus and his message: Professing faith in Jesus is far more than simply assenting to a series of statements of beliefs or following a pattern of certain religious rituals and practices. Earlier in this handbook, faith was defined in a very general way as the sense of trust we have in a power beyond ourselves, in a supreme being or creator of the universe, the one whom we name God. That definition of faith makes sense when speaking of world religions generally. For Christians, however, faith is much more.

Christian faith can be understood as the human response to the unconditional love of God as revealed in Jesus. That response is an intellectual assent to the truth of Jesus' message and a response of the heart and ultimately of the total person. The Christian has fallen in love with God as revealed in the life, death, and Resurrection of Jesus. The church, then, is the gathering of those people who have experienced that love relationship with Jesus and who have joined together to celebrate that love and to support one another in living out that love. The church will therefore be only as strong and loving as the personal faith of its individual members.

A people gathered through the power of the Holy Spirit: Jesus said, "'I am with you always; yes, to the end of time'" (Matt. 28:20, NJB). The gift of Jesus' Spirit at Pentecost was the fulfillment of that promise. As such, the church is not merely a community of people who are trying to live with fond memories of the past. Rather, we are a people who live very much in the present, experiencing and celebrating and growing in our understanding of a God who is here among us right now.

The conviction of Christians is that the Spirit is continually guiding the church, constantly reminding its members of the powerful message of Jesus, and giving them the insight and strength to live according to that message. Granted, the church does not always do a faultless job of responding to that Spirit. At times the church stumbles around in ignorance and selfishness and makes mistakes. In other words, the church remains human with all the strengths and weaknesses of human beings. Perhaps the fact that the church has survived for two thousand years despite its often embarrassing shortcomings is the best evidence that God is definitely with it.

A people gathered to serve others: No dimension of Jesus' message comes through more clearly and directly than his command to love as he loved. Saint John described that command this way:

God is love,
and those who abide in love abide in God,
and God abides in them.

(1 John 4:16, NRSV)

John also says,

Children,
our love must be not just words or mere talk,
but something active and genuine.
This will be the proof that we belong to the truth.

(1 John 3:18–19, NJB)

And again,

Let us love, then,
because [God] first loved us.
Anyone who says "I love God"
and hates his brother,
is a liar,
since whoever does not love the brother whom he can see
cannot love God whom he has not seen.
Indeed this is the commandment we have received from
[Jesus],
that whoever loves God, must also love his brother.

(1 John 4:19–21, NJB)

The implication of these statements both for the individual Christian and for the church as a community of believers is almost frighteningly clear: we can discover and respond to God only in our love for others. The church is a true gathering of Christian people only when its members are reaching out in love to a suffering world. To remain true to its calling by Christ, the church must strive constantly to lessen and eliminate poverty, racism, war, disease, pollution—all those social evils that threaten and destroy so many lives.

This call to battle against social injustice is a very powerful reason for gathering in community. As individuals we are often overwhelmed by the problems of the world. We are painfully aware of how little power individuals possess. If we gather our forces by joining with others, however, we find enormous strength. The Catholic church alone has about one billion members today—that is three times the total population of the United States! Imagine what a tremendous power for good the Catholic church could be if all Catholics became what they are called to be—people professing faith in the Risen Jesus and committed to living lives of loving service through his Spirit. That force for love could change the world! That love force is the dream, the vision, and the prayer of all Christians—and ultimately it is the reason for the existence of the church. If the church avoids that responsibility or loses that incredible vision, it will forfeit its reason to exist.

A Community of Faith Seeking Religious Expression

In our earlier discussion of the nature of religion, we said that people throughout history have apparently shared the need to express their understanding of God in outward, physical, concrete ways. Religion was then defined as the attempt by communities of people to express their shared faith through outward signs—including symbols, celebrations, statements of belief, and codes of behavior. The way these outward signs develop is very much affected by the kinds of symbols and expressions that are available in given cultures and readily understood by the people using them.

The faith revealed by Jesus is incredibly profound and exciting:

- the wonderful mystery of a totally loving God who enters into our human history as a man
- a message of unconditional love for each of us, which in turn frees us to reach out in love to others
- death conquered and a God who is present among and within us for all time
- people called to a community of love, a gathering of people committed to justice and peace

How are such profound ideas and realities to be expressed and shared? How can they be celebrated? How are people to pass on to future generations that marvelous vision that is the message of Jesus? These questions confronted that early community of faith that we read about in the passage from the Acts of the Apostles. What does Luke tell us? That the followers of Jesus "remained faithful to the teaching of the apostles, to the brotherhood, to the breaking of bread and to the prayers . . . [that] they regularly went to the Temple but met in their houses for the breaking of bread . . . [that] they praised God" (Acts 2:42,46, NJB). In other words, they gradually developed religious expressions for the faith that had virtually overwhelmed them with love, joy, and peace and with the need to share that faith with others.

The Religious Expressions of Christian Faith

The attempt by the church to discover religious expressions for Christian faith led to the development of the Christian Testament, to the formal teachings of the church, and to the church's sacraments and other liturgical expressions. In chapter 2 of this handbook we explored the central significance of the Scriptures and Tradition as two distinct ways by which the understanding of Jesus is handed on by the Catholic church.

The Catholic church is also commonly identified by its sacramental and liturgical life. On at least a weekly basis, for instance, Catholics gather for the sacrament of the Eucharist, during which they also hear the Scriptures proclaimed. In addition, they attend Catholic weddings, baptisms, confirmations. Many adult Catholics begin to take these commonplace experiences for granted. Yet a sound understanding of the Catholic church's sacramental and liturgical life is central to a full and rich sense of one's identity as a Catholic. This is a particularly significant point when preparing young people for a fuller sacramental initiation into the life of that community, obviously our chief concern in *Confirmed in a Faithful Community*. Therefore, we now turn to an exploration of this important dimension of Catholic Christianity.

9

Sacraments and Sacred Seasons:
The Worship of the Church

No single characteristic is more identified with Catholicism than its rich public worship and sacramental system. And obviously, the ultimate goal of the entire process of preparation is the joyful celebration of the sacrament of confirmation by the candidates themselves as well as by the entire parish community. Therefore, the theme of this chapter in the handbook—the sacraments and the liturgical year—is of primary importance for all involved in this process.

Reflection session 1 includes an identification activity and a brainstorming exercise on Catholicism in general that may trigger many questions about the sacraments and the liturgical year, questions that then get processed in later reflection sessions. Session 4 explores the nature of sacraments in general, while session 5 concentrates on the three sacraments of initiation, that is, baptism, confirmation, and Eucharist. Session 6 deals directly with the sacrament of confirmation.

The first half of this chapter, in which the general nature of sacraments is explored, will be helpful background for your work throughout the period of reflection. Though the liturgical year— the topic discussed in the latter part of this chapter—is never directly presented in any of the sessions, that material will prepare you for any questions about it that may be generated by the identification and brainstorming activities in reflection session 1 noted above.

Symbols and Celebrations

When Does a Sign Become a Symbol?

We are all familiar with signs that use words. Our days are filled with word signs telling us to stop, to go, and to be careful. Some signs point us in certain directions or urge us to buy certain products that are, in turn, sold inside stores with blinking, neon signs out front. Word signs, as we usually think of them, are a method of communicating simple, direct messages.

Other very familiar signs do not use words at all. These signs speak to us in moving and powerful ways. For example:

- We eat cake routinely, but when we put some candles on a cake, sing a song, and share in fun, a celebration happens!
- A small inexpensive gift takes on much more significance than the cash register can calculate when given to a person for whom we care deeply.
- Jackets that young people wear are ordinary until they put a big letter on them that connects them with something or someone with which they are very proud to be associated.
- The sun sets every day. When we watch a sunset with a loved one, however, the moment is remembered forever.

Such experiences and situations in which apparently ordinary events and objects take on extraordinary meaning are what symbols are all about.

Simple words will not do when trying to convey our more profound and complex messages. For example, when we want to tell someone we love him or her, words are not enough. We need to do something more to communicate the way we feel. Or when we feel great joy, we do not sit down and write about it, we jump up and shout.

This is where symbols come in. A symbol is a special kind of sign that helps us give expression to experiences and meanings that are simply too big for words. Symbols can be either objects or actions. Rings are examples of symbolic objects, just as hugs are often symbolic actions. Some combinations of objects, actions, and words that have particularly rich symbolic value and power are called rituals. To be effective, our symbols and rituals must be similarly understood and valued by all those involved. For instance, a high school class ring found on the street by a grade school youngster may be viewed as valuable in terms of money but not as meaningful otherwise. On the other hand, a birthday cake is a symbol that can be understood and enjoyed by almost everyone.

Natural Events as Sacramental Moments

As the examples of rings and hugs suggest, often we use symbols and rituals in our relationships. Imagine, then, how much more this special language might be needed for expressing the wonderful but often mysterious relationship that people have with God.

For believers, all of nature is a symbol of God's power and love—an expression of who God is and what God wishes for us. So believers can glimpse something of God in even the smallest natural events, for example, a flower's perfume, sunlight on a forest floor, the cry of a baby, the touch of a loved one. No believer can honestly deny that we can touch and be touched by Sacred Mystery when admiring a sunset or enjoying the view from a mountaintop. To deny this is to deny that all of creation is charged with the presence of its Creator.

Whenever Sacred Mystery is revealed in the wondrous and heartfelt moments in life, we can legitimately call these sacramental moments. The word *sacramental* is based on a Latin word meaning "sacred." In other words, these moments are particularly God-charged and so can touch people profoundly, often changing their lives.

Believers in nearly all religions have recognized that some things in nature have particular potential for symbolically conveying profound meaning—meaning that can be immediately sensed by almost everyone. Examples include fire, water, stone, bread, wine, and light. When religions use such things in order to symbolically convey religious significance, these objects are also said to be sacramental.

Having identified the basic nature and power of symbols and rituals to convey religious meaning, we can begin to explore the meaning of those special ritual actions of the church that we call the sacraments.

Sacraments: Celebrations of the Past, Present, and Future

We can easily recognize occasions in life that are so memorable and so profound that we feel an almost automatic need to recognize and celebrate them as sacred. Some obvious examples are a birth of a child, a coming of age when individuals are granted adult freedoms and responsibilities, and marriage. These moments in life are not only special at the time that we first experience them but are so important that we often feel the need to recall and celebrate them for years afterward.

Let's take a nonreligious event as an example. Each year we have birthday parties for ourselves and our loved ones. What are we doing?

- Certainly we are remembering the past event of a birth. We hear the familiar stories surrounding this great moment—the time of day, what the weather was like, any unusual circumstances involved, and so on.
- Yet we are doing more than just remembering that past moment. We are also celebrating what we have become during the years since then. So we talk about how much we have grown—physically, of course, but also mentally and emotionally. In other words, we celebrate who we are now—today.
- We are also looking forward to what we will become or hope to become: "I wonder if I'll get that promotion next year." "Only a few more years and we'll be celebrating our silver anniversary!"

So, along with the past and the present, we look to the future. All the truly memorable moments in our life are celebrated with reference to these three dimensions: we remember the past; we celebrate the present; and we point toward the future.

Historic Religious Events Relived Today

Most religious celebrations are based on the human need to remember profound events from the past, to find ways to celebrate those moments in the present, and to give a sense of promise and hope to the future. Often the historic moments that are being recalled and celebrated occurred for the first time in the life of the founders or of the early believers of the religion. These events, in turn, take on profound significance in the life of later believers.

For example, Passover and Pentecost are two of the Jews' major religious feasts. The historical basis of the feast of Passover was, of course, the escape from slavery in Egypt by the Israelite ancestors of the Jews. The celebration of Passover recalls that historical event, reminds Jews of their personal liberation through the saving acts of Yahweh, and gives the loyal Jew a sense of future hope that one day all the promises of Yahweh will be fulfilled. Similarly, Pentecost recalls the historical giving of the Law to Moses, helps the Jews celebrate their present gratitude for the Law, and enables them to renew their commitment to live out the statutes of the Law in the future.

The major point to be stressed in this discussion is this: The religious rituals we know as the sacraments have three fundamental purposes:

1. to recall profound religious events of the past
2. to allow current believers to realize and to celebrate the significance of those events in their own life today
3. to provide the hope and direction that will sustain believers in the future

Jesus as the Primary Sacrament of the Church

For the early Christian believers—those who walked with Jesus, who lived and ate with him, and who experienced his death and Resurrection—the encounter with Jesus was the most powerful religious event that they had ever experienced. In meeting Jesus, believers gained a tremendous sense of having met God. Certainly many of the people of Jesus' time had already experienced God through nature and through various human encounters, but they had never experienced godliness as fully as they did in this person Jesus. Although many were devout Jews—that is, people who had their own rich history, religious traditions, and sacred memories— they had never encountered God in such an astounding way as they did now.

The Scriptures make it clear that as Jesus taught, preached, and healed both broken hearts and crippled bodies, his impact on the disciples was powerful. Yet Jesus' effect on them was even more profound after they witnessed his death and then experienced him alive again and present among them after his Resurrection. In this experience of Jesus' death and Resurrection, the members of the early church recognized Jesus for the first time for what he truly was: God fully present in human flesh. "'Anyone who has seen me has seen the Father'" (John 14:9, NJB).

So the believers of Jesus' time experienced him as the perfect sacrament of God. That is, Jesus served as the perfect physical, concrete symbol or image of the living God.

After Jesus' time on earth, however, he became present to people in a new way. Now Jesus was present through his Spirit, which continues to enliven and encourage the community of Christian believers. Just as Jesus is the sacrament of God, so the church is the sacrament of Jesus—the outward, physical expression of the Risen Jesus.

The Seven Catholic Sacraments

The church is most clearly recognized as the sacrament of Jesus in its sacramental life. Catholics believe that the sacraments of the church are rooted historically in the life and teachings of Jesus. The sacraments celebrate the past, the present, and the future. They allow Christians to recall Jesus, to "re-present" him—that is, connect powerfully with him in the present—and then to redirect their life in light of his presence. For example:

- Jesus gave an entirely new meaning to the Jewish Passover meal, which he shared with the Apostles at the Last Supper. In the sacrament of the Eucharist, the Catholic church recalls that very special meal.
- The Eucharist is not just a remembrance of a historical event, however. In the Eucharist, the believers who are gathered together share fully in Jesus' presence by sharing the consecrated bread and wine.
- Finally, the Eucharist always points Christians to the future. Nourished by their sharing of the Lord's presence in the consecrated bread and wine, the believers renew their commitment to work toward the unity required if the Kingdom of God is to be fully realized.

Through the centuries, the Eucharist has been surrounded by additional symbols arising from various cultural influences. The basic sacramental action of the shared meal, however, remains unchanged.

Catholics believe that in their sacraments they encounter God's grace in special ways. Grace can be defined as the unconditional and undeserved love of God for people. Catholic Christians believe that the grace of God is nowhere more available and more recognizable than in the church's celebration of its sacraments.

Given all that has been said to this point, we can now define sacraments as they are celebrated by the Catholic church: Catholic sacraments are the religious celebrations through which the community of faith does the following:

- recalls the teachings and actions of Jesus
- experiences the grace of God now present through a personal encounter with the Risen Jesus
- gains confidence and a sense of direction in its efforts to live out Jesus' vision of the future

The Number of Sacraments

As noted earlier in this handbook, one of the historical disagreements between the various Christian churches has been the question of the number of valid sacraments. For example, the Protestant reformer Martin Luther accepted only baptism and Eucharist. He felt that only these two sacraments had clear roots in the Scriptures. Many of the other Protestant churches followed this same line of thought. On the other hand, the Roman Catholic church, relying on Tradition as well as on the Scriptures, gradually identified seven sacraments. Although noteworthy, these different Christian teachings and practices are not nearly as divisive as they once were. Current discussions between Catholics and Protestants display much agreement on many sacramental issues.

In any case, the seven Catholic sacraments flow from the teachings and actions of Jesus as follows:

1. Jesus experienced a particular kind of baptism and later called all his followers to an even more special kind of rebirth. This event is recalled and celebrated in the sacrament of baptism.
2. Jesus sent his Spirit upon people and called them to witness through that Spirit to the presence of a loving God in their midst. Catholics recall that event and celebrate it anew in the sacrament of confirmation.
3. Jesus broke bread and shared wine with those he loved and told them that the bread and wine were his body and blood. In the sacrament of the Eucharist, the church celebrates Jesus' continuing presence.

4. Jesus valued marriage and prayed that nothing would destroy the union of love that Christian marriage celebrates. The Catholic church remembers that value and celebrates the permanent union of man and woman in the sacrament of marriage.
5. Jesus recognized that some persons have a very particular role to play in the life of the community of faith, a role of leadership and of a particular kind of service. Catholics recall that value and celebrate it in the sacrament of holy orders, the special anointing of the priesthood.
6. Jesus constantly forgave others and called all his followers to the same willingness to forgive and accept those who may fail in their efforts to love. In the sacrament of reconciliation, the Catholic church remembers that attitude, celebrates the liberation from sin of its members, and reaches out to others.
7. Finally, Jesus healed the sick and promised his followers that not even death could keep them from the fullness of life that he was offering. Catholics remember that promise and face their own sicknesses and death with the strength gained from the sacrament of the anointing of the sick.

All these profound values and teachings are celebrated through the rich and powerful symbols of the sacraments. As a result, Catholics move into their future as stronger, better, more hopeful Christians.

More Than Memories of the Past

An essential concept in the Catholic understanding of the sacraments is that they are not simply recollections of past events but rather re-presentations of those events in the life of believers today. Jesus died nearly two thousand years ago, but he was also raised from the dead, and he promised that he would be with us "'always; yes, to the end of time'" (Matt. 28:20, NJB). Jesus is present, here, among us.

Catholics believe that in the sacraments and in a special way in the consecrated elements at Mass, the Risen Jesus is present more clearly than at any other time. In other words, the sacraments do what religious symbols are meant to do: they allow persons to reach to the depths of life rather than merely bob on its surface. Catholics believe that the seven sacraments help them reach to the depths of their faith experience of Jesus and, there, to meet God.

The Communal Experience of the Sacraments

Earlier we learned that symbols and celebrations can be truly effective only if they are understood and valued by those persons sharing them. Imagine, for example, a birthday party at which most of the guests are strangers who barely know the one celebrating her or his birthday.

The same can be said of the sacraments: They are God-charged moments that can touch people and change their life, but only if people have "the eyes to see and the ears to hear," as Jesus said. Those Catholics who experience the sacraments as empty and meaningless might check to see if their understanding of the sacraments is correct and complete.

We turn now from our concentration on the celebrations that make up the sacramental life of the Catholic church to a discussion of the annual cycle of religious feasts and seasons that serves as the broad context of the communal worship of Catholics.

Celebrating with Sacred Seasons

God Revealed in Nature

Imagine yourself as a cave dweller living tens of thousands of years ago. Put yourself in the place of a prehistoric hunter out alone at dusk, gazing in wonder at the moon's rising, yet having none of our modern scientific explanations for what is happening. As an early human, how would you explain the mysteries of creation?

We can begin to find an answer to that question by reflecting on how people typically react to natural events. When a snowfall blankets the earth, bringing with it incredible beauty and deep stillness, we will often hear people say, "God, how beautiful!" Similarly, when the springtime sun warms skin that has been covered for months by winter clothing, Northerners especially will sigh, "My God, how good it is to be alive!" When a long-awaited rainstorm eases the pain of a drought, farmers immediately want to shout, "Thank God!"

Even when nature seems to turn against humanity, people find the hand of God at work. A hurricane smashes into an island and kills thousands. A volcano spews forth molten lava, burning and crushing homes in its path. A tornado rips apart a neighborhood. An earthquake devastates whole sections of a city, leaving thousands dead or homeless. In response, people search their heart and mind for answers to the haunting question, "Why? My God, why?"

If the workings of nature can put modern people in touch with Sacred Mystery, we can begin to appreciate the religious response of prehistoric peoples to such events: our early ancestors saw gods at work behind every event in nature. In fact, most religions—early or modern—have been sensitive to the revelation of God within nature.

Developing a Sense of Time

As history progressed, people recognized nature's cycles. That is, they became increasingly conscious of the repeating seasons and of the predictable movements of the sun, moon, and stars. Based on their observations of natural cycles, people slowly developed the notion of time. The idea that ancient people did not know about time may seem impossible. In our society, we are so concerned about being "on time" that imagining a historical era in which no sense of time even existed is hard for us to do. Yet the whole notion of time only gradually developed out of people's growing awareness of natural cycles as well as out of their changing social needs. For example, when humans took up farming, they had to determine the best time to plant and to harvest crops to avoid the risk of damage by floods or frosts. Our familiar units of time developed along the following lines:

The day: Throughout history the notion of a twenty-four-hour day evolved, based on observations of the sun. For us, the official start of a day is midnight, but this was not always the case. Originally the day was measured from one sunrise to another or from one sunset to another. Jewish holy days, for example, last from one evening to the next. Then again, we often talk about the morning as the start of a new day.

The week: Eventually early cultures began to think in terms of larger units of time than days. The concept of a seven-day week, for example, was based mainly on the Jewish story of Creation, which is found in the Bible. According to this story in the Book of Genesis, God created the world in six days and then rested on the seventh. This led the Jews to establish the weekly holy day called the Sabbath, from the word for "rest." We will have more to say about the Sabbath a little later.

The month: The unit of time that we call a month was based on observations of the moon's changing phases. The lunar cycle lasts approximately twenty-nine and one-half days. So the earliest unit that we now call a month included either twenty-nine or thirty days. Throughout history, many religious observances have been linked to this monthly cycle. As we shall see later, our modern approach to determining the date of Easter is directly related to the lunar cycle.

The year: When people gradually recognized the need for a longer unit of time than the month, the answer seemed obvious. They could add up enough lunar months to make a year. The problem was that lunar cycles do not match the cycle of the seasons. Eventually the lunar calendar for a year would fall out of step with the growing seasons. Clearly, another natural cycle was needed that would be a more practical and predictable standard for figuring out when to plant or harvest crops. People eventually realized that the position of the earth in relation to the sun follows a constant pattern. Based on this predictable cycle, then, a period of 365 days became the unit of time that we call a solar year. Days were then added to the lunar months to fit them to a solar year.

Religions and the Passage of Time

Why discuss the cycles of nature, the changing seasons, and the evolving concept of time? The reason is that almost all religions have developed major religious celebrations centered on their central beliefs and on key moments in their histories. These celebrations are, in turn, often linked to the cycles of nature. The result is an annual cycle of religious celebrations that are considered sacred days or sacred seasons.

Occasionally a religion will take a nonreligious festival or the celebration of another religion and give it a new religious significance. For example, we earlier noted the Jewish feast of the Pentecost. Before the Jews existed as a people, this was a springtime festival celebrating the harvest of the winter crop. Jewish rabbis then began to associate this celebration with the giving of the Law to Moses on Mount Sinai. What was once a celebration with little religious significance thus became an important religious feast. As we will see in a moment, the Christian celebration of Christmas has a similar history.

The Liturgical Year of the Church

The church has evolved a complex series of religious seasons and special feasts based on the life, death, Resurrection, and Gospel message of Jesus. Although not organized on the basis of our modern solar calendar, these seasons and feasts do follow an annual cycle. The purpose of this cycle of worship is to help Christians to daily touch the very heart of their faith—the mystery of Jesus of Nazareth, risen and alive among us today. This annual cycle of religious feasts and seasons is known as the church's liturgical year. The word *liturgy* is based on a Greek word meaning "public." So the term *liturgical* refers to the public or communal worship practiced by a religion.

As part of this discussion of the church's worship, we will explore in a general way how the liturgical seasons and holy days of the Catholic church unfold throughout the course of the year. More specific information on each season will be provided later.

The Liturgical Year at a Glance

As we begin this discussion of the Catholic church's liturgical year, take a moment to reflect on the chart of the annual cycle of seasons and major feasts provided on page 155. Doing so will provide a good sense of how the seasons and feast days flow from one to another throughout the course of the year.

Just as our solar year is divided into units of time—that is, days, weeks, months, and seasons—so the liturgical year is also divided into recognizable units of time. The church year includes five major seasons that unfold in this order:

- Advent
- Christmas
- Ordinary Time, which is divided into two parts—the first part falls between the Sunday after the Epiphany and the start of Lent; the second part follows Pentecost
- Lent
- Easter

The Liturgical Year

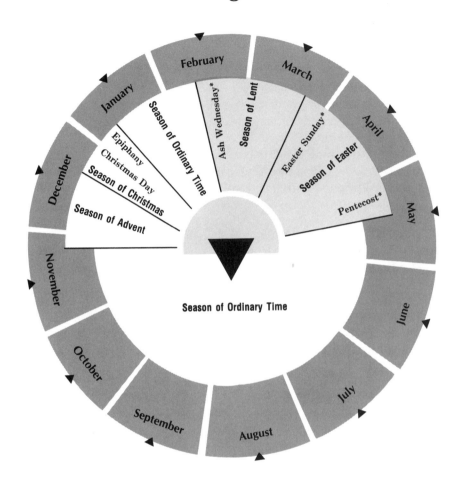

*Easter falls anywhere from late March to late April. So the dates for Ash Wednesday and Pentecost also vary from year to year.

Within this annual cycle, many individual days celebrate particularly important events in the life and ministry of Jesus.

- Every Sunday is dedicated to Jesus and the memory of his death and Resurrection. We will discuss Sunday worship more fully later on.
- Certain Sundays are recognized as particularly significant, as are a few weekdays during the year.
- Most of the weekdays of the year are dedicated to the memory of saints who in special ways witnessed to the Gospel values of Jesus.

Following are some insights into the specific days and seasons of the church year, insights that can make our experience of the church's liturgy more rich and satisfying.

The Liturgical Year: A Closer Look

The Season of Advent

Keep in mind in our discussion of the church's liturgical year that our normal calendar year and the liturgical year of the church do not begin at the same time. We immediately think of the new year as beginning on 1 January. The church's liturgical year, however, begins with the season of Advent, which starts four Sundays before Christmas. During these weeks the church prepares to celebrate the coming of Jesus by focusing on scriptural themes related to the coming of the Messiah.

The Season of Christmas

The season of Christmas begins, of course, with the joyous celebration of Christmas Day on 25 December. As a whole, this season continues the celebration of the early life of Jesus and the growing awareness by the early church of his identity as the Son of God. As early as the fourth century, the church recognized and celebrated Christmas as a special day. Remember the comment earlier that the Jewish feast of Pentecost had its roots in a relatively nonreligious celebration? Our celebration of Christmas also has borrowed some of its characteristics from non-Christian customs. Perhaps by coincidence, the celebration of Christmas fell about the same time as the Roman feast of the "Invincible Sun" and some customary observances based on the position of the sun in the midwinter sky. Out of this mix of cultural and religious practices, Christians developed such customs as giving gifts, decorating homes with greenery and lights, and so on. Even the symbol of the Christmas tree has its roots in pagan custom.

The Christmas season closes with the feast of the Epiphany. The word *epiphany* is based on a Greek word meaning "manifestation." On this day and during the period immediately following it, the church celebrates the first awakenings of people to the special identity of Jesus as God. In the Western church—that is, the Christian church of which most Christians of Western cultures are members—the Epiphany emphasizes the first recognition by non-Jewish people of Jesus' identity. This is represented by the Gospel story of the Magi's visit to the infant Jesus.

The Season of Ordinary Time

At this point in the church's liturgical year we have the first part of the season of Ordinary Time. This lasts from Epiphany to the beginning of Lent, and that length of time can vary depending on when Easter falls in a given year. During Ordinary Time, which is also known as simply the Season of the Year, the church concentrates on the life and teachings of Jesus rather than on the central events of his birth and Resurrection. Individual Christians reflect on those qualities of Jesus that should characterize their daily life.

The Season of Lent

The fourth major season of the church's liturgical year is Lent. Lent begins with Ash Wednesday, which occurs forty days before Easter Sunday, not counting Sundays. Lent reminds Christians of two events: the forty days Jesus spent in prayer in the desert following his baptism in the Jordan River, and the forty years the Israelites wandered in the desert following their escape from slavery in Egypt. A solemn time during the church's cycle of seasons, Lent helps Christians recall and reflect on all the events that led up to the world's rejection and ultimate execution of Jesus. As individuals, believers reflect as well on those areas in their life where they have failed to live out the values of Jesus.

Yet Lent is not meant to be a totally sad time. Rather, the primary purpose of Lent is to help the church and its individual members properly prepare for the celebration of the central Christian mystery—the Resurrection of Jesus. Lent, therefore, does not celebrate pain and suffering, but rather the inevitable triumph of life and hope over death and despair.

The season of Lent has particular relevance in regard to the celebration of confirmation. Historically, Lent emerged out of the early church's complex catechumenal approach to the initiation of new members. The third period of that process, known as the period of purification and enlightenment, was a time of intensely prayerful immediate preparation before the reception of the three sacraments of initiation—baptism, what we now know as confirmation, and then Eucharist. The catechumenal approach to initiation has been recovered by the contemporary church with the promulgation of the Rite of Christian Initiation of Adults (RCIA) in 1972. The church now requires that *all* initiation of new members today—including the celebration of confirmation among adolescents—must be grounded in the theology of the RCIA. That is why in *Confirmed in a Faithful Community,* the third period of the preparation process, which we call the period of reflection, immediately precedes the Rite of Confirmation and has a particularly prayerful and reflective quality and focus. The period of reflection tries to capture, in ways appropriate to the contemporary adolescent, the earliest and central meaning of Lent—prayerful preparation for full initiation into the community of faith. (See part A of the coordinator's manual for *Confirmed in a Faithful Community* for a thorough discussion of the history and theology of the initiation process.)

The Season of Easter

Easter Sunday, the most important feast in the church's cycle of worship, is the start of the fifth major season of the church's liturgical year—the Easter season. Just as the Jewish feast of the Passover is a great springtime feast for the Jews, so the central Christian feast of Easter is celebrated in the spring of the year, the time of new life. Easter does not fall on the same day each year as do Christmas and Epiphany. For complicated historical reasons, Christians celebrate Easter on the first Sunday following the first full moon of springtime. This can fall anywhere from late March to late April. Curiously, a part of our worship is still linked to the changing phases of the moon. Churches in our day are attempting to arrive at a standard day of the year on which to celebrate Easter.

The Easter season lasts for fifty days and is a period of great joy and hope. During this time, the readings at Mass focus on the disciples' encounters with Jesus following his Resurrection from the dead. The entire church, it seems, is joined in spirit with Thomas, the Apostle who initially doubted that Jesus had been raised and who later joyfully exclaimed in meeting him, "'My Lord and my God!'" (John 20:28, NJB).

The Easter season lasts until the feast of Pentecost, which is celebrated on the Sunday that falls on the fiftieth day after Easter. Pentecost, of course, celebrates the coming of the Spirit upon the group of frightened disciples who had gathered following the death and Resurrection of Jesus. Traditionally it is said that the church was born on that day, a church that nearly two thousand years later continues to celebrate these marvelous events.

The Season of Ordinary Time—Revisited

The second phase of the season of Ordinary Time begins the day after Pentecost and lasts until the beginning of Advent and the start of a new year in the church. Several of these weeks of Ordinary Time focus on the divinity of Jesus. The last Sunday of the year, for instance, celebrates the feast of Christ the King. During the closing weeks of Ordinary Time, the church celebrates the belief that the Risen Jesus will one day come again in glory. In other words, Christians renew their sense of awaiting the coming of the Lord. The spirit of the church's worship during this season is perhaps best summed up by the very last words of the Bible:

The one who attests these things says: I [the Lord] am indeed coming soon.

Amen; come, Lord Jesus.

May the grace of the Lord Jesus be with you all. Amen.

(Rev. 22:20–21, NJB)

So at the close of the liturgical year, Christians renew their sense of awaiting the coming of the Lord and, in that spirit, enter into Advent. And the marvelous cycles of the liturgical year begin anew.

Sunday:
Christians Dedicate the Week to God

Special mention must be made of the central role of Sunday Eucharist in the church's worship. Christians throughout the world and since the earliest days of the church have recognized the obligation of believers to worship together on the first day of each week. Many Catholics are so accustomed to following this practice that they may not even know where it comes from. So let's briefly explore the origins of Sunday worship.

It was noted earlier that the Jews consecrated their week to God through Sabbath worship. From early in their history, the Jews have regarded the Sabbath, which extended from sunset on Friday until nightfall on Saturday, as a sacred time. Absolutely no work of any kind was allowed on this day of rest. During their pre-Christian history, some Jews even allowed themselves to be slaughtered rather than break the Sabbath laws by taking up arms against their enemies. When we hear of the commandment to "keep holy the Sabbath," we must remember this history to gain a sense of the importance of this law in the minds of the Jews.

Most of the earliest Christians were, of course, Jews. After they had experienced the Resurrection of Jesus on the first day of the week—what we know as Sunday—they almost immediately began to gather on that day each week to celebrate the Resurrection and to prepare for what they expected to be the almost immediate return of the Risen Jesus. For a time, many of the Jewish converts continued to attend Sabbath worship with the Jews and then joined with Christians for worship on Sundays.

This Christian worship on Sunday was very simple compared with what Christians experience today. Believers gathered in small neighborhood communities for prayers and the breaking and sharing of bread. The worship would often take place very early in the morning because Sunday was an ordinary workday at that time, and many Christians had jobs; also, the act of gathering at the time of the rising sun to honor the Risen Son was a strong symbol in itself.

In the beginning, these weekly gatherings were celebrations of Easter. Only when Christians realized that the Risen Lord would not be returning soon did they set aside one Sunday of the year as a special celebration of the Resurrection. Naturally they associated the Resurrection with the Jewish feast of Passover. So, even today, these two religious holy days occur at nearly the same time every year.

Parts of the Jewish synagogue service were gradually incorporated into Sunday worship. Later, as the Christian Testament began to emerge, readings from it also became part of the worship. Throughout the centuries, of course, the celebration of the Mass has taken on ever greater complexity. Incidentally, since 1967 the Catholic church has considered the time period from Saturday evening through Sunday as appropriate for attending a Sunday Mass. This change reflects the original Jewish understanding of a day lasting from one sundown to the next.

Right from the beginning of Christianity, Sunday worship was recognized by believers as a very special responsibility. Society did not acknowledge Sunday as a special day, however, until a Roman emperor, in the fourth century, accepted Christianity as the official religion of the state. At that time, Sunday was established as an official day of rest for the entire Roman Empire. This practice remains somewhat true to this day, at least to the extent that most people do not work on Sundays.

Today Catholic Christians of all ages frequently question the value of Sunday worship. Many reasons are given for this attitude—among them a reluctance to attend Mass merely out of a sense of obligation. Rather than treating Mass as a question of duty, however, believers might be more in touch with the spirit of Sunday worship if they recalled its profound and beautiful history. For when Christians gather for worship now, they are in a very real and wonderful way gathering in spirit with their fellow believers from the earliest days of the church until the present. As always, they gather in the sure conviction that they do so not only in the name of the Lord but also in the Lord's very presence. "'For where two or three meet in my name,'" promised Jesus, "'I am there among them'" (Matt. 18:20, NJB).

Community Worship and Personal Spirituality

The worship of Catholic Christianity is complex and occasionally confusing. This should not surprise us, growing as it does out of nearly two thousand years of complicated church history. Remember also that the church's sacramental and liturgical life was founded upon more than a thousand years of Jewish history and worship.

In closing this discussion of Catholic worship, we must recall that the experience of faith and religion is both communal and deeply individual. On the one hand, Catholics share a very real bond with nearly one billion other Catholic believers. Wherever they gather across the globe, they all share essentially the same beliefs, celebrate the same seven sacraments, and relive in the liturgy the life, death, and Resurrection of their Lord.

On the other hand, each believer experiences a unique journey of gradual conversion to the Lord. Often a Catholic person's sense of participation in the life of the community is directly affected by what she or he is experiencing in terms of personal faith development.

We rightly concentrate a great deal in *Confirmed in a Faithful Community* and, therefore, in this handbook on the communal dimensions of Catholic Christianity. We have discussed the nature of the church, explored the significance of its Scriptures and Tradition, and reflected upon its worship. As we now move to bring both this handbook and the process of preparation to a close, we need to turn to focused reflection on the more individual dimension of Catholic Christianity. For if the Catholic faith is to have any true meaning for its members, it must speak to the hearts of believers as they grapple with the everyday issues of the Christian life:

- How can I grow in my own personal relationship with God?
- What does meeting God in prayer mean, and how can I do that in a way that satisfies me?
- What guidance can Catholic faith offer me as I confront the difficult issues of my daily life?

Questions such as these are the focus of the period of mission in *Confirmed in a Faithful Community,* and they are the subject as well of the next and final chapter of this handbook.

10

Growing
in Catholic Christian Faith:
A Love Relationship with God

The integrating theme for the period of mission is living in the Spirit of Jesus. A common question posed by newly confirmed young people is, How can I keep this feeling alive? When asked to describe what they mean by "this feeling," many will speak of a closeness to both God and the church, a sense of spiritual vitality, a feeling of integrity and wholeness. What they are seeking, I believe, are the fruits of a maturing personal spirituality. Both the mission sessions themselves and this closing chapter in the handbook try to define and describe what constitutes the personal spirituality of growing Christians.

In this chapter Christian spirituality is discussed in terms of a slowly developing and deepening love relationship with God in and through Jesus. After an exploration of the analogy between faith in God and human love relationships, four elements for growth in Christian spirituality are thoroughly considered: a growing knowledge of the Gospel of Jesus, a deepening of that knowledge in prayer, ongoing involvement in a supportive community of faith, and engagement in loving service to others.

Christian Faith as a Love Relationship with God

Earlier in this handbook we discussed religious faith as a sense of trust that people have in a power beyond themselves, in a supreme being or creator of the universe whom we call God (see chapter 1). We considered faith as a deeply personal relationship that people experience with their God. We then said that Christian faith is the human response to the unconditional love of God revealed in Jesus. We noted, "That response is an intellectual assent to the truth of Jesus' message and a response of the heart and ultimately of the total person. The Christian has fallen in love with God as revealed in the life, death, and Resurrection of Jesus" (chapter 8, page 137).

If Christian faith, then, is at root a love relationship with God, we can learn much about the dynamics of faith growth by reflecting on our experience with other love relationships. Additionally, by approaching this discussion of the process by which we grow as Christians from the perspective of other love relationships, we can connect concepts that are potentially quite theological and philosophical with the lived experience of the candidates.

The Character of Human Love Relationships

To analyze the complexity of human love relationships is not our intent here. Doing so would require another book! Rather, we want to use the most basic and simple understanding of love relationships as a kind of metaphor for the kind of relationship between God and the believer that we have identified as faith. Four traits seem to occur in the development of virtually all love relationships:
1. The relationship often begins on a special note.
2. The persons then grow in knowledge of each other.
3. That knowledge leads to a commitment.
4. Finally, the commitment to love is continually renewed and deepened.

Note that these characteristics, though seemingly universal, will be expressed differently depending on the nature of the particular love relationship under consideration: between parent and child, between good friends, between romantic lovers, and so on. Yet the characteristics of love relationships are reflected in each of these particular love relationships.

A Special Start

It may seem superfluous to note that all relationships begin somewhere or in some way. However, the *way* in which one meets another can become a significant factor in that love relationship. In some cases, the first meeting sets a special tone for the relationship. Married couples, for example, often look back at their first meeting as a case of love at first sight. Something clicked in their minds and hearts that made marriage later on seem a natural result.

This fundamental characteristic of love may seem a little difficult to identify if the love relationship under consideration is between a parent and a child. How can children say that they "meet" their father or mother? Yet even in such cases we often speak of truly "meeting" a parent or a sibling only quite late in life, recognizing that all our earlier contacts with each other were on the surface or were strained for one reason or another. The fact is, all love relationships involve recurring meetings, often accompanied by the feeling of starting all over again.

A Growing Knowledge

Next, all love relationships involve a process in which the parties gradually get to know each other. This aspect of all love relationships can be delightful but is often difficult. With people like one's parents, this growth in knowledge is so gradual and long term that one may not even be conscious of it. In other cases, one may be able to recall in some detail the entire process of growing in knowledge of the other. All love relationships include this kind of growing knowledge and understanding.

An Eventual Commitment

Another characteristic of all love relationships is that they require decisions and commitments. Even in family relationships this is true because simply living together is no guarantee of the presence of love. Parents have to demonstrate very clearly that they love their children. In the same way, children eventually arrive at a point when they must decide whether to respond to that love or to reject it.

Many people have found that the full experience of love for their parents is only possible when they themselves become independent adults. The reason is that love demands freely made decisions. That kind of freedom is difficult to experience when one is dependent on parents for food, clothing, and shelter.

So love relationships demand a freely made commitment. In the case of a relationship with a best friend or spouse, one may even be able to identify the time when that commitment was made in a very clear and even dramatic way.

A Continual Growth

Finally, love relationships must continue to develop and grow or they will inevitably weaken and die. A marvelous characteristic of lasting love is that it can continually grow because the two people never stop growing themselves and never stop discovering new things about each other. The longer we care for someone, the more aware we are that each human being is an infinite and changing mystery.

Christian Faith as a Love Relationship

What does this discussion of the stages or key characteristics of love—admittedly oversimplified—mean in terms of a faith relationship with God? The point is simple yet profound: if Christian faith is a response to the love of God, it shares many of the characteristics of every other love relationship. We have seen that although each relationship we experience is unique, our friendships and our other love relationships share common characteristics or patterns of development. We meet another person, we grow in knowledge of the other, we make a decision to respect and care for the other, and then the relationship grows deeper. So it is with Christian faith. Certainly each person experiences a unique relationship with God. Yet common characteristics seem to exist in a faith relationship with God.

Christian Faith Begins Somewhere

Obviously faith must begin by somehow meeting God. For Christians, baptism marks God's presence offering the gift of faith, but exactly when a person consciously meets God may not be easily remembered. As in a child's relationship with a parent, the origins of an individual's faith relationship may be hidden in a cloudy past. This is particularly true when a family exposes a young child to many outward expressions of faith. Such expressions may include meal prayers, bedtime prayers, stories about Jesus, examples of Christian conviction by parents. These childhood experiences of faith can be so much a part of family life that a person never becomes fully conscious of their importance.

On the other hand, someone who recently became aware of the presence of God—perhaps through a very powerful religious experience of Sacred Mystery—will often be able to identify precisely when his or her faith became real and recognizable. This stage in the development of a faith relationship with God might be what some Christians identify as the moment of conversion, the point at which they can say they met Jesus.

Christian Faith Requires Knowledge

Once a conscious faith relationship with God begins, a believer's knowledge of God must continue to grow. Catholic Christians often learn about God from their parents and then gradually become more involved in the larger religious community. Typically, Catholics celebrate Eucharist in the parish; listen to the reading of the Scriptures; experience the sacrament of reconciliation and, perhaps, the sacrament of confirmation; attend weddings and baptisms; and so on. Young Catholics may also attend formal religion classes, either in a Catholic school or in a parish program. Slowly the knowledge of God and of Christian faith grows and matures.

Remember another point that has been stressed in *Confirmed in a Faithful Community:* Faith in God is not simply an intellectual issue; it is also a matter of the heart. Formal religious education and religious celebrations within a community of believers offer marvelous insights into God. Yet these insights must eventually be confirmed in a person's private perspective on life—in reflecting on her or his life experiences, in encountering God in the wonders of creation, in sensing Jesus' Spirit within human relationships, and so on. Once a Christian acquires a personal worldview in which Jesus is Lord, she or he is ready for the next stage in the development of faith.

Christian Faith Demands a Commitment

The stage of decision or commitment is that time—perhaps an identifiable moment but more commonly a certain period or span of time in one's life—when the Christian assumes personal responsibility for living according to the values of the Gospel. A very important point must be made in this regard: Just as one cannot be forced to love another person, so one cannot be forced to love God or to decide to be a Christian. Every Christian arrives at this moment on a unique schedule and by a unique route.

Additionally, a personal faith commitment will be reflected differently in different persons, with the response often affected by one's personality type. So we have to avoid stereotyping what Christian commitment looks like and presuming that we can easily identify when an individual arrives at it. For instance, some falsely assume that a commitment to Jesus requires an emotionally charged response of some kind. Such narrow expectations can lead to unfair judgments of others. Even worse, if held by leaders of pastoral programs, such narrow concepts of commitment can lead to manipulative if not dangerous approaches in which the leaders try to force individuals to respond in the prescribed manner.

Finally, the meaning of Christian commitment clearly becomes a matter of serious concern in the context of preparation for confirmation. What kind or level of commitment can reasonably be expected of the young candidates participating in *Confirmed in a Faithful Community*? The coordinator's manual discusses that question at some length. Suffice it to say here we can expect no more of the young people than God would. And God only expects each of us to be true to who we are and can be at any point in our life. That may mean for some young people that their confirmation commitment to Jesus will be tentative, filled with doubt and questioning . . . and perfectly acceptable to God.

Christian Faith Keeps on Growing

Once the decision is made to accept the love of God, the love relationship that we call faith becomes a lifelong process of continual growth and development. As is true with other love relationships, growth in faith will not always be easy. This growth includes both high points and low points, moments of great joy and moments of severe doubt, times of intense closeness to God and times of great loneliness.

Yet this growth process is not boring and routine. Faith in God lived out with conviction and openness is exciting and fulfilling. "'I have come so that they may have life,'" promised Jesus, "'and have it to the full'" (John 10:10, NJB). The believer knows that Jesus is true to that promise. In Christian faith, the believer is involved in a love relationship with Sacred Mystery—with a God whose infinite wonder and love expels boredom.

The Tasks of Growing in Christian Faith

If Christians are to continually grow in their faith, they must take on the following four tasks:

1. Christians must constantly seek better knowledge of the meaning and message of Jesus.
2. They must then deepen their understanding through personal prayer.
3. They must also support and gain encouragement from other believers in the community of faith that is the church.
4. Finally, Christians must reach out in loving service to the people around them.

These four tasks—centered on knowledge, prayer, community, and service—are at the heart of growth in Christian faith. Let's explore each of these in greater depth, especially noting how they might be lived out by the adolescent candidates.

Growing in Knowledge of Jesus' Life and Message

A growing love relationship requires a constantly expanding understanding between the people involved. The initial knowledge that one gains of a person can lead to the commitment of love. That love in turn often drives a person to seek more understanding of the loved one.

The same is true about faith in God: A basic knowledge about Jesus and his message is required before the personal decision about faith can be made. Yet after that decision has been made, an almost unquenchable thirst for more knowledge develops. How do Christians grow in their knowledge of Jesus? To whom do they turn for more information?

The Bible as a primary source of knowledge: Earlier in *Confirmed in a Faithful Community,* we discussed at some length the central place of the Bible, particularly the Christian Testament, as a primary source of information about the message of Jesus. Reading the Bible with guidance, either by using sound study guides or by studying in the company of others who are recognized for their knowledge of and background in the Scriptures, is particularly useful. However, this legitimate emphasis on the need for directed study should not keep any Catholic from private reading of the Scriptures.

Where should a young person start when learning to read the Bible? One of the Gospels—preferably Mark's or Luke's—would seem most appropriate. If, after reading either one or both of these, she or he wants to continue the practice of regularly reading the Bible, perhaps the young person should then ask a teacher or parish leader for a guided reading program. Many good ones are available.

If the thought of regular Bible reading does not appeal to the candidates, encourage them to take fuller advantage of the times when the Bible is read *to* them, particularly during the Mass. Urge them to listen as carefully as they can to what is read. They might try to carry on a silent dialog with the priest during his homily, asking themselves if they agree with or could add to his insights about the readings.

The community of faith as a source of knowledge: Perhaps the most influential sources of information about the faith are simply other Christians who are willing to share their experiences. Christianity is not simply knowledge about someone or something. Rather, it is essentially a way of living, a life stance that is based on a growing love relationship with God. Many people are involved in this ongoing journey of faith—parents, teachers, and friends. Getting to know other Christians, listening to their stories of faith, and sharing one's own experiences with them can be an invaluable source of growth in the understanding of faith.

A comment might be added here as well about a characteristic of Christian spirituality that is particularly Catholic. The Catholic church emphasizes more than other Christian churches a conviction in the *communion of saints.* This term refers to the entire community of believers, both living and dead.

Christians at work in the world today offer loving service to others—service that deeply impresses even those who are not Christian. The inspiring work of Mother Teresa among the dying people of Calcutta, India, has rightly received much attention by the media. Yet each of us has likely met Christians whose goodness is so transparent that we would acknowledge them as saintly even if the world generally never honors them.

In their respect for holy people, however, Catholics more often revere saints who have died in service to the Lord. One dimension of the Catholic church's liturgical year that we did not emphasize in our previous discussion is what is called the church's *sanctoral cycle*. The Catholic church celebrates most weekdays as the feast days of particular saints. In its daily liturgies, the Catholic church honors the memory of these individual saints who serve as striking models of faith for today's believers.

Because of their high regard for the saints of the past, Catholics have occasionally been accused of worshiping saints. Some people have suggested, for example, that instead of praying to God, Catholics pray to saints, especially to Mary the mother of Jesus. This interpretation of the Catholic understanding of the saints is inaccurate. Catholics do not venerate the saints *instead of* the Lord. Rather, Catholics look to and honor the saints *because of* what the Spirit of Jesus has accomplished through these special people. By looking at the works of the saints, Catholics discover both direction and encouragement as they work out a personal faith relationship with God.

Life as a source of knowledge: One's personal life experience is another vital source of knowledge about God and faith. God loves constantly and reveals Sacred Mystery within life experiences. Reflecting on the glad and sad moments in daily life, being sensitive to world events, and then praying over these personal and social happenings in quiet reflection can provide a tremendous amount of insight about the journey of faith. Exercises like the keeping of a personal journal can help a great deal in this regard. All in all, the opportunities for growing in understanding of Jesus and his message are limited only by the imagination and the ambition of the individual. This growing knowledge is essential to the ongoing development of faith.

Deepening Knowledge Through Prayer

For a long time in the history of the Catholic church, the most common definition of Christian faith was that it was an assent to truth, that is, an intellectual acceptance of the teachings of Jesus. As we have stressed throughout *Confirmed in a Faithful Community*, the church now teaches that such a view of faith in God is too narrow, too restricted to the intellectual level of life. Christian faith is much more than a mental exercise through which a person becomes comfortable with philosophical formulas and arguments. If faith in God were only that, a person's ability to grow in faith would be completely dependent on his or her level of intelligence. Nothing could be further from the truth.

Believers need to learn as much as possible about faith, but if faith remains on the level of intellectual beliefs, it is not faith in its fullest sense. Faith in God must go much deeper than the mind; it must touch the depths of the heart. The usual way that faith touches a person at this level is through the experience of prayer.

Prayer is often thought about in the rather restricted sense of talking to God or saying prayers—as if prayer were simply a matter of repeating words in the hope that someone out there is listening to them. Thinking of prayer in a much fuller and more personal sense can help to improve our attitudes toward it.

Prayer is sometimes defined as communication in a relationship of love. The word *communication* indicates that prayer is not a one-way process in which a person simply talks to God. Rather, communication implies that what is shared in prayer is a two-way exchange or dialog. In a prayerful dialog, the person shares her or his thoughts and feelings but also receives some feedback—that is, some kind of response from God. How does this happen?

The answer has much to do with the fact that the communication within prayer takes place within a relationship of love. People in love communicate in all sorts of ways, not just with words. Many times, in fact, words seem almost to get in the way of communication between friends. For example, many of us have had the experience of simply sitting for a long time in the presence of a friend without saying a thing. We might listen to music together, take a long walk in silence, or sit quietly by a lakeshore or on a hill, sharing a beautiful view. Does communication take place in such situations? Sure it does: we leave these encounters with friends feeling refreshed and also feeling closer than before.

Prayer works in a similar way. Some kinds of prayer, in other words, do not require words, and yet they are fulfilling dialogs rather than one-way monologs. We might ask, however: How does a person know that God listens? How does God talk back to the person praying? Let's explore some possible answers to these important questions.

Why bother to pray? The conviction of believers is that God speaks all the time, communicating Mystery and inviting a response from people during each moment of their life. The conviction that this is so is based purely on the belief that God truly loves us as individuals. Consider this: If you love someone, you need to be with that person, to share, to express yourself to him or her. If God loves, that love demands these same expressions.

If we do not believe that God loves us as individuals, of course, the whole idea of prayer becomes ridiculous. Why bother? God certainly does not need our nice words. If God does not care about us, all the talk in the world is not going to change the situation.

If we do believe that God loves us, on the other hand, not praying—not opening ourselves to the power and joy of a love that is without limits—would be silly.

Daily life as the content of prayer: Because God loves each person individually, prayer must also be personal, unique, and centered on individual life experiences. So prayer can be a kind of dialog with God simply about how life is going, about feelings, and about other relationships. We share these kinds of things in all love relationships.

How does God answer prayers? God generally does not respond to one's prayer with a booming voice from out of a cloud! God responds to people in their inner selves and their inner needs, because it is on that level of their life that they reach out to God. Consider the following examples:

- An attempt at prayer can open a person's mind and give her or him a better vision of life. God's response in prayer might be a clearer perception of what one's life is all about, where a person is going in life, and so on.
- God gives the power to live according to what one knows in the heart is true. Therefore God in prayer can touch the will and strengthen a person's character.

- God calms the emotions in the experience of prayer, and prayer can bring peace to a confused mind and heart.
- God in prayer can fire the imagination with new ideas, new possibilities, new ways of dealing with the world.
- Finally, God can communicate through memories, allowing a person to learn from past mistakes and to gain the encouragement needed to move into the future with hope.

A believer can do much to improve prayer. Exercises can be done, bodily positions can be assumed to help one pray, disciplined routines can clear one's mind for prayer, and so on. An in-depth discussion and practice of such methods is beyond the scope of *Confirmed in a Faithful Community.* The key principle to remember here, however, is that prayer is not only the recitation of memorized prayers at specific times and only in buildings constructed for that purpose. On the contrary, a person can pray all the time, simply by being in touch with daily life experiences and by trying to see God in them. God loves us constantly, and because of that love, God is with us all the time—loving, caring, and asking for a response in faith. Prayer is an essential part of that response and an essential part of growth in Christian faith.

Sharing Faith with the Community of Believers

The third dimension of a growing and deepening Christian faith is the practice of joining with others in the community of faith for mutual sharing, support, encouragement, and celebration. Jesus taught that faith in God is not to be a one-to-one relationship. In other words, Christian faith is not a matter of each believer living in isolation and pursuing a private relationship with God. Faith is ultimately a communal experience—an experience that must be shared with others if it is to mature. That is precisely why the church exists.

Christians have been called to live in community for two primary reasons:

1. The message of God's love promotes a sense of celebration. The believer has a desire to reach out to others in joy. When something great happens to us, we want to have a party, to get all the gang together to share our good fortune. This urge to celebrate one's blessings is one of the impulses for participating in the church, the community of faith.

2. The actual living out of the message of Jesus can be very difficult. Trying to be all we can, trying to care for others, can be
plain hard work, which cannot be done without the help of others who share our convictions. So the encouragement and support of other believers is vital.

These two reasons also serve to explain why the Catholic church so
strongly emphasizes the need for its members to gather for regular
worship. The purpose of the weekly celebration of the Eucharist is
not only to fulfill the duty to worship God. The Eucharist is also an
opportunity for believers to celebrate their lives as Christians and
to rededicate themselves to support one another in their mission to
heal a suffering world.

The church is believers, not buildings: The official gatherings of the church are very important. Participation in the life of
the church takes place most visibly and directly through the sacramental life of the church discussed in chapter 9. The sacraments
allow Catholics to gather in community to reflect on and celebrate
the key events in their life—the very events in which they can discover God.

Yet the church is not simply a place where people go to do certain things. Participation in the life of the church takes place wherever believers live and act as persons of faith. Whenever Christians
care for others, whenever they reach out with concern to those
around them, the church is present.

Parish life as a center of communal faith: Catholics en-
gage in the sacraments primarily in parishes, which are often small
communities that allow believers to get to know one another, to
feel part of the same life experiences, and to develop friendships
with one another. The parish also provides many opportunities beyond the sacraments and the other liturgical expressions of the
church. Examples include social events, service projects to help
those in need, and a variety of programs to respond to specific
needs in the parish. All these are opportunities for involvement in
the community that we call church.

A final note on this dimension of Christian faith: the parish
community will only be as alive as the faith of its members. Many
people, unfortunately, view their parish communities as spiritual
service stations. They go to Mass on the weekend to get filled up
with enough spiritual fuel to get through the week.

This approach ignores the fact that people fuel the parish. The parish community is one in which individuals who are already growing in their faith come together to share the fruits of that experience and to celebrate it with others. People must participate in parish life, therefore, with an attitude of giving as well as getting. Strangely enough, the more that parishioners give, the more they grow in faith.

Reaching Out in Service to Others

Finally, Christian faith demands that believers seek personal growth for more than their own happiness and that of their local community. Indeed, the entire thrust of the message of Jesus is that Christians must always be using their talents to reach out to a wounded world—a world that desperately needs the healing touch of love.

Too many Christians feel that they are responsible only for themselves and for their own development. They figure that if they avoid doing bad things, they have done all that is asked of them. This is simply not the case. Christian faith is more than avoiding the bad. Rather, it is a matter of doing the good by stretching beyond one's own interests to help others. A major part of this attitude of service is a sincere concern that all people be treated with justice. Everyone must do as much as possible to alleviate the monumental problems of world hunger, for example, and to work toward the time when the world can truly live in peace.

Christian Faith and Christian Morality

A brief comment can be made at this point about a central issue in Christian faith: Christian morality. Morality generally deals with decisions about right and wrong behavior. Christian morality deals with these issues in the context of Jesus' teaching about God's love and the human response to that love. We live in a world in which many Christian values have been seriously challenged. Young people today confront enormous difficulties with issues such as sexual promiscuity, the abuse of alcohol and other drugs, violence, cheating in the classroom, and so on. The burden on all those who are sincerely trying to live according to Christian values can be immense.

We do not have the time in *Confirmed in a Faithful Community* to deal at length with these kinds of issues. A full understanding of and appreciation for Catholic Christian moral values and their impact in the lives of believers requires much investigation and discussion. We can only hope that the candidates at some point in their future formation have an opportunity for an in-depth exploration of Christian moral principles.

Yet some very basic information on the meaning of Christian morality can be provided here. For example, people who sincerely strive to develop their personal faith along the lines presented in this chapter will be virtually guaranteed lives of moral conviction. In fact, true Christian morality cannot be understood apart from this commitment. The ways Christians choose to act in their daily life directly reflect their belief that God unconditionally loves them and that they can best respond to that love by caring for others. Christian morality is, then, a result, or an end product, of a commitment to live out these values.

Making Moral Decisions as a Christian

In striving to make good decisions about tough moral issues, Christians look for guidance outside themselves as well as within their own heart. The following material attempts to summarize both dimensions of the process of decision making. The process is presented to and discussed by the candidates during the period of mission.

Step 1: Define the Issue

Begin by defining the issue at hand as clearly as possible. In some cases, such as abortion or the morality of capital punishment, this may require considerable study and reflection. In other cases, such as stealing or destroying property, the issue may be more easily understood.

Step 2: Seek Advice

After defining the issue, look for outside resources for information and guidance. Among those resources are the following:

- the values and teachings of Jesus as found in the Christian Testament
- the formal teachings of the church, especially those things that the church regards as always being wrong
- the advice of respected people who possess deep faith and obvious goodwill

Step 3: Reflect Honestly on the Consequences

Reflect on the morality of certain actions, decisions, and attitudes in light of the results they are likely to cause. The next two paragraphs provide examples of the results of moral and immoral decisions.

Actions, decisions, and attitudes are right or moral when they produce all or some of the following results in the one acting or in those who are affected by the actions:
1. an increase in the ability to trust others
2. greater honesty in all relationships
3. a lessening of the sense of separation
4. an increase in an attitude of cooperation
5. a greater sense of self-respect
6. a stronger belief that people are generous and caring
7. a feeling of peace and joy in life

Actions, decisions, and attitudes are wrong or immoral when they produce all or some of the following results in the one acting or in those who are affected by the actions:
1. an increase in suspicion
2. a feeling of phoniness in all relationships
3. a feeling of isolation or loneliness
4. an increase in useless competition
5. feelings of guilt and embarrassment
6. a stronger belief that people are greedy and selfish
7. a feeling that life is lousy

Step 4: Pray for God's Guidance

In prayer, the believer weighs the results of all the reflection suggested by the previous steps. The Christian asks God to guide him or her to do what is right and to reject what is wrong.

Once the Catholic Christian has seriously considered a decision in light of guidelines such as these, she or he can act with confidence. Does this seem like a lot of work? Certainly. Yet, those who care enough to work at their moral decisions are able to live in dignity and peace.

A Final Word

This brings to a close this handbook for catechists. It was designed to provide the kind of basic theological background that might simplify but also make more enjoyable your work with *Confirmed in a Faithful Community.* I hope that it has also whetted your appetite for even deeper explorations of the wondrously rich heritage that is ours as Catholic Christians.

What a tremendous responsibility—but also great gift—it is to say yes to the invitation to help pass on the Catholic Tradition to another generation of believers. In doing so you are joining with that early community of Christians who, in experiencing the Resurrection, were moved by the Spirit of Jesus to proclaim the Good News.

Acknowledgments *(continued)*

The scriptural passages cited as NAB are from the New American Bible with Revised New Testament. Copyright © 1986 by the Confraternity of Christian Doctrine, Washington, D.C.; and the New American Bible, copyright © 1970 by the Confraternity of Christian Doctrine. Used with permission.

The scriptural passages cited as NRSV are from the New Revised Standard Version of the Bible. Copyright © 1989 by the Division of Christian Education of the National Council of the Churches of Christ in the United States of America.

The scriptural quote on page 122 is from the Jerusalem Bible. Copyright © 1966 by Darton, Longman and Todd, London; and Doubleday, a division of Bantam, Doubleday, Dell Publishing Group, New York.

Much of the material in this handbook has been adapted from two Saint Mary's Press textbooks by Thomas Zanzig: *Jesus of History, Christ of Faith*, 1992, and *Understanding Catholic Christianity*, 1988.

The version of the Nicene Creed on pages 42–43 is from *The Sacramentary* (New York: Catholic Book Publishing, 1985), page 368.

FSU BOOKSTORE

MAR 0 4 2022